THE LIVING WHITE HOUSE

White House

THE LIVING WHITE HOUSE

Betty C. Monkman

Published with the support of the Hon. Walter H. Annenberg

White House Publications Fund

White House Historical Association

Washington, D.C.

Editions 1–10 were produced by the National Geographic Society as a public service.
Original Author: Lonnelle Aikman

12th Edition

ISBN 0-912308-97-4

Library of Congress Control Number 2006934329

Opposite: Sheep eating
on the South Lawn of the White
House during the presidency of
Woodrow Wilson, 1919.

Page ii: A stereoview made
of the north side of the White
House in the 1860s captures
pedestrians on Pennsylvania
Avenue.

Page vi: President and
Mrs. George W. Bush
dance at the Commander-
in-Chief Ball celebrating his
second inaugural, 2005.

Page vii: Tourists form a
line along E Street on the
south side of the White House,
1962.

THE WHITE HOUSE

The White House is often called the "People's House," and in these pages you will learn about the people and events that have shaped America's most famous residence.

President Bush and I visited the White House often when his father, George H. W. Bush, was president. With so many warm memories, when President Bush and I moved into the White House, it already felt like home. And that's what the White House is: a home for the president and his family, and a symbolic home for America.

The White House has witnessed weddings and births, wars and celebrations, and important milestones in the lives of some of our nation's most remarkable men and women. Here, President Lincoln planned how he would preserve our Union. President Nixon delighted in the union of his family and President Eisenhower's. From the Diplomatic Reception Room, President Franklin Roosevelt broadcast his historic Fireside Chats. President Theodore Roosevelt's children amused White House staff with their games and exotic pets.

Today, President Bush and I work to preserve the history and traditions of the White House as we make a home for our family. We host foreign leaders at State Dinners, and invite friends for informal lunches. We have decorated our personal rooms with family photos, and restored the original décor of the Lincoln Bedroom. We exercise on the South Lawn, read books in our living room, and watch our Scottish terriers play in the snow.

We also love having guests. In 1805, President Thomas Jefferson opened the White House to tours, and today the halls are filled with visitors eager to explore this living museum. Children gather here every spring for the Easter Egg Roll, and summertime brings the South Lawn Sluggers for afternoons of tee ball. Thousands of visitors come every year to tour the gardens, where they view seasonal displays of tulips, magnolias, and chrysanthemums in bloom.

From old traditions to new, the White House has evolved with every president and his family. Today it endures as a testament to history, and a symbol of our great democracy. President Bush and I encourage you to learn more about this historic home in the pages of *The Living White House.*

Laura Bush

CONTENTS

FAMILY MEMBERS AND DESCENDANTS OF PAST PRESIDENTS POSED WITH FIRST LADY LADY BIRD JOHNSON AT A WHITE HOUSE CEREMONY TO CELEBRATE THE PUBLICATION OF THE FIRST EDITION OF *THE LIVING WHITE HOUSE* IN 1966.

Seated are: Julia Grant Cantacuzene (granddaughter of President Grant, born in the White House); and Marthena Harrison Williams (granddaughter of President Benjamin Harrison). Standing from left are, Sistie Seagraves (granddaughter of President Franklin Roosevelt); First Lady Mamie Eisenhower; Ellen Douglas Gailor Cleveland (daughter-in-law of President Grover Cleveland); Mrs. Johnson; Marion Cleveland (daughter of President Cleveland); Lawrence Hoes (a descendant of President Monroe); Mary Eisenhower and Barbara Ann Eisenhower (granddaughters of President Eisenhower); Elliott Roosevelt (son of President Franklin Roosevelt); Susan Eisenhower (granddaughter of President Eisenhower); Mary Virginia Devine (great-granddaughter of President Benjamin Harrison, daughter of Marthena Harrison Williams); Irene and John Roosevelt (daughter-in-law and son of President Franklin Roosevelt); and Helen Taft Manning (daughter of President William Howard Taft).

FOREWORD

"A president and his family cannot forget that they have joined the stream of history, that the home they occupied briefly, living their family life, is also an American showplace. . . . Through everything they do runs the consciousness that here throbs the heart of a great and powerful nation," explained Lady Bird Johnson upon the publication of the first edition of *The Living White House*, the book that she inspired, in 1966.

This, the twelfth edition of *The Living White House*, celebrates the beginning of a special book's fifth decade in print. The text has been updated by former White House curator, Betty C. Monkman, who began her nearly forty-year career during the administration of President Lyndon B. Johnson. Having served eight presidents, Ms. Monkman herself is a part of the life and history of the White House, and her contribution sets this edition apart. The story of the life of the President's House cannot be fully told without pictures, and with this new edition we have taken the opportunity to enlarge the design and include more than two hundred new and historic images. Many are recent archival discoveries that have never before been published, and many are familiar favorite photographs from past editions, which after decades of wear, have been revived with the latest in printing technology.

The White House Historical Association first published *The Living White House* with the cooperation of the National Geographic Society to serve as a companion to *The White House: An Historic Guide,* which focuses on the decor and furnishings of the house. During the past forty years, eleven editions and more than 1 million copies have been printed. Every first lady to follow Lady Bird Johnson—Patricia Nixon, Betty Ford, Rosalynn Carter, Nancy Reagan, Barbara Bush, Hillary Rodham Clinton, and Laura Bush—has maintained her original enthusiasm for telling the story and has generously assisted with each updated printing. We are again grateful to Mrs. Bush and her staff for their assistance with this new edition.

We welcome you to the White House and to this book of which we are so proud.

Henry A. Dudley Jr.
Chairman of the Board of Directors

PREFACE

When the White House Historical Association began to plan a new edition of *The Living White House,* I was delighted to be asked to assist with its reorganization and the revision and updating of the text. In thinking about a new approach to the book with association president Neil W. Horstman, director of publications Marcia Anderson, and editorial consultant Ann Hofstra Grogg, it seemed that this popular book would be of more value to the reader if it were organized by thematic topics reflecting the various roles of the White House over two hundred years: office of the president of the United States and his staff; center of the nation's hospitality; home of the president and his family; special gardens and grounds; and historic residence—its changes, renovations, and staff. These subjects are illustrated with many new historic and contemporary images.

Much of the text remains that of its original author, Lonnelle Aikman, with whom I had the pleasure of working on several editions. Many people have contributed to this edition. At the White House, the staff of First Lady Laura Bush including her chief of staff, Anita McBride, speechwriters Ed Walsh and Meghan Clyne, and the White House Photo Office rendered much assistance, as did William Allman and Lydia Tederick of the White House curator's office, and Claire Faulkner of the chief usher's office.

At the White House Historical Association, Marcia Anderson guided the publication with skill and excellent suggestions, and Vanessa Piccorossi and Sharon Pierce were very helpful with text revisions. Harmony Haskins and Hillary Crehan assisted with photographic research and compilation.

Ann Hofstra Grogg contributed editorial advice and several valuable recommendations to the book's new structure and text. A fresh new design was created by Marilyn Worseldine. At Peake Delancey Printers, LLC, James Brooks and Debbie Buckey-Hoffman worked to ensure the quality of the images.

It has been a pleasure to have worked with the excellent staff on this revised edition. Our goal has been to create a thematic, visually attractive publication that would convey the broad scope of life and work in the President's House.

Betty C. Monkman

Children rush to gather eggs at the Easter Egg Roll on the South Lawn of the White House, 1929.

The President's House, The Nation's House

The White House is part of every American's national heritage. As the office and home of the president, it is the place toward which citizens look for leadership from the person they have chosen to act for all. No other elected official is so directly accountable to them. Their problems are his problems; his home is theirs.

John Adams, the first chief executive to live in the White House, once wrote, "People of the United States! You know not half the solicitude of your presidents for your happiness and welfare." "I never forget," said President Franklin Delano Roosevelt in one of his famous fireside chats, "that I live in a house owned by all the American people and that I have been given their trust."

The Executive Mansion has been a focal point of government and a barometer of the political, economic, and social state of the nation ever since it was first occupied in 1800, a decade after Congress had established the country's permanent capital in the fields and forests beside the Potomac River. It has known the tramp and flames of enemy invaders, the pomp of victory celebrations, the pain of economic depressions, the private joy of family weddings, and the somber pageantry of state funerals.

Unlike the ornate and monumental palaces of Europe's royal past, the porticoed White House stands today with simple dignity amid green and rolling grounds in the heart of Washington. Since John and Abigail Adams became its first residents, forty-one presidents and their families have lived in this very public building, where hundreds of official events are held each year and thousands of guests and visitors walk through its public rooms and grounds. As author Lonnelle Aikman wrote in the first edition of this publication, "Indeed, it is this personal and domestic life, carried on in the fierce glare of national affairs, that gives the White House its fascinating dual character."

A morning view of the White House across Lafayette Park, 2007.

Presidents at Work in Their Home

1

The White House, whose long-popular name was not officially
inscribed on the presidential letterhead until Theodore Roosevelt's
time, stands as a living symbol of the nation's power and prestige.
As the home and office of the chief executive, it is the keystone of the
government. With Congress and the Supreme Court, it is the central
theater of action in which national goals are achieved and defended.
But the fascination the White House holds for most Americans is in its
association with the great men who helped create the United States.

President William Howard
Taft signs legislation in
an Oval Office ceremony
authorizing statehood for
Arizona, February 14, 1912.

BUILDING THE FIRST WHITE HOUSE

WASHINGTON D.C. 1798

THE PRESIDENTS

Opposite: In this 1930 illustration entitled *Building the First White House,* by N. C. Wyeth, George Washington is depicted with architect James Hoban at the White House construction site. Although he oversaw the design of the building, Washington was the only president who did not live in the White House.

Above: George Washington's portrait was painted by Gilbert Stuart in 1797 and placed in the White House in 1800. Rescued by First Lady Dolley Madison, it is the only object that has remained in the collection since before the British set the White House on fire in 1814, during the War of 1812.

George Washington, though "Father of His Country" and "first in the hearts of his countrymen," was the only president who never lived in the White House. He ended his service as chief executive and died before the federal government moved from Philadelphia to the village capital named in his honor. Even so, Washington left the indelible mark of his own dignity and good taste on this eighteenth-century building with its magnificent setting. He selected its site and gave his prestigious approval to the classical, harmonious design for the mansion submitted by Irish-born architect James Hoban in a democratically open competition. In envisioning the home in which the presidents would live, Washington expressed his vision for the future of the new country: "For the President's House, I would design a building which should also look forward, but execute no more of it at present than might suit the circumstances of this Country when it shall be first wanted. A plan comprehending more may be executed at a future period when the wealth, population, and importance of it shall stand upon much higher ground than they do at present."

From the beginning the "President's House"—the name Washington preferred—was destined to be a stage for events that marked the progress of the nation from a dozen states stretched along the Atlantic seaboard to a preeminent world power reaching into the Pacific Ocean. Here President Thomas Jefferson, in his first term, accepted Napoleon's offer to sell the

French-owned port of New Orleans and
the vast lands to the west known as the
Louisiana Purchase. James Madison faced
a far more painful decision in the War of
1812 – called "Mr. Madison's War" by his
foes. At the darkest hour of the conflict,
when Dolley Madison and the cabinet were
in flight from the burning capital, the president must have wondered if he had endan-
gered all that the Revolution had won.

To the President's House in 1829
came tough Andrew Jackson, hero of the
battle of New Orleans. "Old Hickory" was
the first man to reach the top executive
office from the open frontier beyond the
Appalachians. His overwhelming presidential victory in 1828 clearly demonstrated the new political power of a grow-

ing and more democratically based elec-
torate, and it alerted the aristocratic states-
men of the East that henceforth national
leadership would be shared with the people of the West. The campaign of William
Henry Harrison rolled to success in 1840
on a bandwagon bearing twin symbols of
a log cabin and a barrel of hard cider,
despite the fact that Harrison was not
born in a log cabin but was a scion of
Virginia aristocracy and had no special
taste for cider.

Two decades later, Abraham Lincoln
bore the burdens and heartbreak of the
"irrepressible conflict" of the Civil War
in the vortex of the struggle. Through
bitter military reverses and petty partisan
politics, in the face of cruel criticism and

cartoons picturing him as a clown and a devil, he held together the frayed bonds of union until the nation could again be united.

"I think of Lincoln, shambling, homely, with his strong, sad, deeply furrowed face, all the time," Theodore Roosevelt wrote a friend after he, too, came to live and work in this house of historic memory. "I see him in the different rooms and in the halls . . . he is to me infinitely the most real of the dead Presidents."

Harry Truman recalled his predecessors, too. "I sit here in this old house and work on foreign affairs, read reports, and work on speeches. . . . The floors pop and drapes move back and forth—I can just imagine old Andy and Teddy having an argument about Franklin."

The men who have taken on their country's toughest assignment reflect many different backgrounds. Together their varied lives support the democratic proposition that every American, however humble in origin, has a chance to reach the highest position in the land. Abraham Lincoln was born in a log cabin, as were several other chief executives. The exact number is uncertain because the claim of humble origins—authentic or not—had potent political appeal in frontier days.

Eleven presidents were former generals—including George Washington and Dwight Eisenhower. Warren G. Harding was a newspaper publisher; Herbert Hoover was an engineer. Several presidents were teachers or college professors.

On July 4, 1861, President Abraham Lincoln reviewed Union troops from a platform erected on Pennsylvania Avenue on the north side of the White House.

At least twenty practiced law early in their careers; many served as state governors, members of Congress, and cabinet officers.

Eight vice presidents rose to the presidency on the death of incumbents; four of them—Theodore Roosevelt, Calvin Coolidge, Harry S. Truman, and Lyndon B. Johnson—went on to win another term on their own. Gerald R. Ford was the only vice president to attain the office by the resignation of a chief executive. He replaced Richard M. Nixon, who resigned under threat of impeachment by Congress.

William Howard Taft, defeated for a second term in 1912, was later appointed by Harding to be chief justice of the United States—the only man ever to serve in both high posts. Of the two, Taft preferred the

Supreme Court. "I don't remember that I was ever President," he once remarked happily.

In view of the frantic nature of many election campaigns, it is amazing that there has never been an interruption in the lawful exchange of residents at 1600 Pennsylvania Avenue. One potential disruption followed the election of 1876, when Samuel J. Tilden won the popular vote but neither he nor the other candidate, Rutherford B. Hayes, secured the necessary majority in the Electoral College. Returns from four states were disputed. With the opposing parties deadlocked, an Electoral Commission chosen by Congress decided in favor of Hayes. Because of the dispute and because March 4, then the legal inauguration day, fell on Sunday, Hayes took the oath of office in a private White House ceremony on March 3 while attending a dinner given by outgoing President Ulysses S. Grant. Few of the dinner guests were aware of the event when President Grant quietly led the other principals into the Red Room, where Hayes was secretly sworn in by Chief Justice Morrison R. Waite. The formal inauguration took place peacefully at the Capitol on Monday, March 5. Another potential disruption following the election of 2000, in which neither Al Gore nor George W. Bush could secure the necessary majority in the Electoral College without the votes of Florida, where returns were disputed, was resolved by the Supreme Court. Again the inauguration, by this time moved to January 20, was peaceful.

Above: Harry S. Truman takes the Oath of Office in the Cabinet Room upon the death of President Franklin D. Roosevelt, April 12, 1945.

Left: President Gerald Ford takes the Oath of Office in the East Room after the resignation of President Richard Nixon, August 9, 1974.

THE PRESIDENT IN HIS OFFICE

President Abraham Lincoln
with his secretaries
John Hay and John Nicolay,
November 8, 1863.

Wherever the president goes, his office goes with him. His work is never done, whether he is editing a speech aboard his well-equipped plane or reading the latest of his daily reports at midnight in his study or his bedroom. The president's day-to-day duties are with him always, and they have steadily increased since John Adams complained that a "peck of troubles in a large bundle of papers . . . comes every day."

As the nation grew from some 5 million people in 1800 to more than 280 million in 2000, each new president has inherited heavier and more complex duties and responsibilities. Behind the stately pillars of the Executive Residence, as in the inconspicuous East and West Wings and in the nearby executive office buildings, where most official business goes on, staff members help their chief meet his obligations, great and small. Their tasks include assisting the president with his political and legislative agendas, planning domestic and national security policies, gathering and analyzing information, receiving visitors, handling correspondence and documents, and preparing for a constant round of official and social activities.

When John Quincy Adams took on the presidency, the growing paperwork was made almost unbearable by his failure to delegate it. To cope with the minutiae, he used shorthand no one else could decipher, and he impaired his eyesight and health by writing thousands of words a week in official and personal correspondence.

James K. Polk was similarly inclined. "No President who performs his duty faithfully . . . can have any leisure," he declared. "If he entrusts the details . . . to subordinates constant errors will occur. I prefer to supervise the whole operation of the Government myself." Already, however, this had become impossible. Polk's attempt to do the task put such a strain on his frail constitution that he became ill and died at age 53, a few months after leaving office.

Congress was slow to provide funds for executive help. Most early presidents called on a relative to act as private secretary, paying salaries from their own pockets. Congress finally voted money to hire one private secretary for President James Buchanan; then the Civil War suddenly increased the need.

Lincoln acquired two bright and talented young secretaries, John Hay and John Nicolay, and clerks detailed from other government departments. But no one could shield the president from the burdens of a country at war, nor would he permit himself to be sheltered from the avalanche of problems unloaded by officials, generals, war contractors, cranks, wounded soldiers, and tearful wives and mothers.

Until 1902, when President Theodore Roosevelt built the West Wing to separate

Clerks at work in the Staff Room, the largest room in the West Wing, in 1908. Correspondence was a major responsibility; as many as one thousand letters were received each day.

his office from his living quarters, all families shared the Executive Mansion with the public, which was freely admitted to ask favors, to seek interviews with the president, or just to shake his hand. Most annoying was the clamor of petitioners for

Outgoing President Grover Cleveland leaves his successor Benjamin Harrison holding the door in this 1889 cartoon deriding the seemingly endless flow of office seekers demanding the chief executive's time.

public office, often raised by those without qualifications. Lincoln told of a man who asked for a post as a foreign minister and gradually reduced his demands until he was willing to settle for an old pair of pants. Office seekers, however, had become pests long before Lincoln's administration. They and their eager sponsors haunted the White House even in the time of John Adams. With each change of administration came fresh hordes, and president after president complained of persecution and senseless waste of time. Jackson openly used the spoils system to reward his supporters. For a time fear stalked the ranks of his opponents in government service; in all, it is estimated, about one-fifth of the entire workforce

was replaced. During William Henry Harrison's tenure, a group of men once barred him from a cabinet meeting until he accepted their applications. Yet it was not until after James A. Garfield's murder by a thwarted job hunter that firm action was taken. In 1883 Congress passed the Pendleton Act, the first major reform law to open the way to competitive examinations as the basis for most federal service. The nation was coming of age. Such changes in public attitude toward the obligations and rights of the man in the White House reflected the increasing energy, wealth, and population of the country.

Gone are the days when Grover Cleveland could write many of his letters and speeches by hand, or when William McKinley and his staff of a dozen people could cope with all of the business. Woodrow Wilson sometimes picked up a letter from a secretary's desk and answered it on his own typewriter. Harding was the first president to hire a professional speechwriter. Computers were introduced into the White House during Richard Nixon's tenure and came into widespread use under Jimmy Carter.

As the problems have increased and grown more complex, the presidential staff has come to include domestic, legal, and national security advisers at the White House, plus economic, technical, and other advisory groups in the neighboring executive office buildings. Late twentieth-century presidents and the first presidents of the twenty-first century, supervising the nerve center of action in the West Wing,

Above: President William McKinley dictates to his secretary, J. Addison Porter, at the Cabinet Room table where he liked to work, 1897.

Left: A White House messenger on horseback, c. 1890 and a White House courier, 1906.

have found that the pace of their work has grown ever faster with new technology.

Theodore Roosevelt carried out his dynamic foreign and domestic programs in a period when messengers on horseback or bicycle rushed urgent letters and documents to and from the White House, Congress, and executive departments. Automobiles came in with Taft. Harding was the first president to broadcast a speech by radio. Truman was the first to deliver an address from the White House by television. The first airplane assigned to the chief executive was a specially built C-54 used once by Franklin Roosevelt, and later by Truman. Jets and helicopters have been supplied since Eisenhower's time.

Back in 1877 Hayes installed a telephone at the mansion after seeing one demonstrated by inventor Alexander Graham Bell. Yet as late as Taft's term only one operator was needed to handle calls. When the operator went to lunch, Taft's young son, Charlie, considered it great sport to take over the switchboard. Today many telephone operators routinely take thousands of calls a day, and e-mails flood the White House, from those expressing their opinions on current issues and those seeking assistance from the president.

To their regular schedules, presidents in this century have added travels abroad. Theodore Roosevelt was the first president to leave the United States, traveling to Panama in 1906. Wilson was the first to go to Europe, attending the peace conference at Versailles following World War I. Franklin Roosevelt was first to visit South America and Hawaii, and he attended the historic World War II conferences at Casablanca, Tehran, and Yalta. Truman went to Germany for a conference at Potsdam, held just before the war's end. Since the age of jet travel, presidents have traveled extensively throughout the world for international conferences and state visits.

When formulating and promoting policies, most presidents have shown a high regard for the people's support and understanding. "I shall go just so fast and only so fast as I think I'm right and the people are ready for the step," said Abraham Lincoln. Benjamin Harrison declared that public opinion was "the most potent monarch this world knows." Indeed, public opinion often may weigh more heavily in a president's decision than advice from his cabinet. Chief executives have varied sharply in consulting department heads on important matters—a choice left open by the U.S. Constitution. James Monroe conferred at length with his cabinet, and especially with Secretary of State John Quincy Adams, before pronouncing the Monroe Doctrine that warned European powers against further expansion in the Western Hemisphere. Andrew Jackson, on the other hand, largely bypassed his cabinet, preferring to discuss issues with friends, who were disparaged as his "kitchen cabinet" but who served him capably and loyally.

Even during the First and Second World Wars, Presidents Woodrow Wilson and Franklin D. Roosevelt seldom called a cabinet session. Roosevelt, like Jackson, chose to confer with outsiders of differing views and with some of his administrative assistants whose qualifications, he said, were "high competence, great physical vigor, and a passion for anonymity."

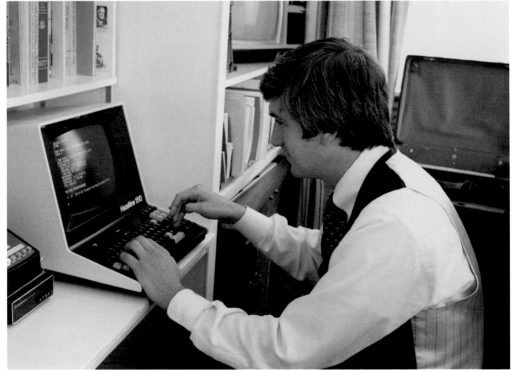

Above: A White House teletype operator at work, 1909.

Left: Personal computers were introduced during the Carter administration, 1978.

Above: President Ulysses
S. Grant with his cabinet,
1869.

Right: President Theodore
Roosevelt's last meeting
with his cabinet, March 2,
1909.

Above: President Lyndon B. Johnson with his cabinet, 1966.

Left: President George W. Bush sits between Secretary of Defense Donald Rumsfeld and Secretary of Homeland Security Michael Chertoff in a cabinet meeting following Hurricane Katrina, August 31, 2005.

THE PRESS

Over the years, the public image projected by every president and his family has been part fiction and part reality, part personal and part official. The more forceful the president, the more distinct his image. Cartoons of Teddy Roosevelt, for one, with his toothy grin and round glasses, evoke the earnest conservationist who helped preserve the nation's natural resources and the indomitable David who fought the Goliaths of industrial monopoly. But the president is not always able to control his image, because news coverage follows him wherever he goes. Teams of reporters check his daily appointments, quiz him on policy at press conferences, and accompany him on travels. The news media follow the president's wife with equal scrutiny.

As an institution, the press conference began when Wilson initiated formal question-and-answer meetings with reporters to explain his programs. It has continued in varied forms, from requiring reporters to submit written queries to the present rapid-fire questioning under television lights. Originally held in the Oval Office, the conferences were moved to the Executive Office Building during the Eisenhower administration. Now they usually occur in the East Room or West Wing and sometimes in the Rose Garden.

Press accommodations have come a long way since reporters had to pick up what news crumbs they could from outside the mansion's entrance. Theodore Roosevelt provided the first White

Opposite: Reporters gather around President Franklin D. Roosevelt's desk for a press conference, August 25, 1939.

Above: President Gerald R. Ford holds a press conference in the Rose Garden, October 9, 1974.

Above: President Ronald Reagan answers questions from the press in the Press Room in the West Wing, August 4, 1986.

Right: President Bill Clinton calls on a reporter at a press conference in the East Room in 1999.

House newsroom in his new West Wing, reputedly after taking pity on reporters shivering in a winter storm. Further improvements were made in 1970, when a press center was built over Franklin Roosevelt's swimming pool. It includes a briefing room and two floors of booths for writers and broadcasters.

In a world of dire emergencies and instant communications, the White House has become a focal point of the fierce, incessant searchlight of global attention. To meet the demand to know what goes on here, some one-hundred reporters and photographers—from newspapers, magazines, television, and radio—regularly cover activities of the president and first lady. Nearly two thousand others have credentials and attend special events, such as visits of foreign officials.

Above: President George W. Bush holds a press conference in the East Room, 2004.

Left: The press reports from Pebble Beach, just off the North Lawn of the White House, on a snowy day in 2004. The Eisenhower Executive Office Building is in the background.

President George W. Bush walks in the snow across the South Lawn with his dog Spot, December 2002.

THE LONELIEST PLACE

In the morning Franklin Pierce had been escorted to the Capitol by the outgoing chief executive, Millard Fillmore. At noon Pierce delivered his inaugural address before a cheering crowd and rode to the White House, where for hours he accepted the congratulations of well-wishers. It was growing late when the last handshaker departed. The house was in disarray, with stacks of soiled dishes and chairs pushed in all the wrong places. The servants had disappeared. Jane Pierce, mourning the recent death of the couple's only child to survive infancy, was still in New Hampshire. Wearily, President Pierce, climbed the stairs by candlelight with his private secretary, Sidney Webster. He was president of the United States, and he stood at the pinnacle of a political man's career. But he was alone.

Taft called the White House "the loneliest place in the world." John Quincy Adams remembered his years at the White House as "the four most miserable" of his life. "What is there in this place," cried James A. Garfield, who was hounded by office seekers and would soon be murdered by one, "that a man should ever want to get in it?" "I enjoy being President," Theodore Roosevelt wrote to his son Kermit, "and I like to do the work and have my hand on the lever." But, after one year in office he confessed, "Everyday, almost every hour, I have to decide very big as well as very little questions, and . . . what it is possible . . . to achieve." For Jefferson, the presidency was "a splendid misery"; for Jackson, "dignified slavery." For Truman, the President's House was "a great white prison." On his desk

Right: Secretary of State
William R. Day signs the
Peace Protocol of the
Spanish-American War
in the Cabinet Room,
as President William
McKinley and others
watch, August 12, 1898.

Below: President Harry
S. Truman announces
the surrender of Japan,
August 14, 1945.

stood a sign that read, "The buck stops here."

No matter the support from family and advisers, nothing can relieve the president of the sole responsibility of decision making. With word and act, he marks his place in history when he signs or vetoes a bill on economic affairs, for instance, or when he proposes a foreign aid program or issues an order for military operations abroad. "No easy matter will ever come to you," Eisenhower told President-elect John Kennedy on the eve of the 1961 inauguration. "If they're easy they will be settled at a lower level."

The weight of the president's obligations is never so starkly displayed as when his decision alone sets his country on a path of life or death, peace or war. Facing such a challenge, McKinley wept, said a confidant, in pouring out his troubles in the Red Room during the frantic days before the Spanish-American War. Wilson's call for a declaration of war against Germany followed sleepless nights of assessing the consequences. After Truman took the awesome responsibility of using the atomic bomb against Japan in World War II, he wrote in his autobiography that he "regarded the bomb as a military weapon and never had any doubt that it should be used." But then came the perilous week in 1962 when the United States and the Soviet Union stood "eyeball to eyeball," H-bombs ready. Kennedy had made his

President John F. Kennedy meets with his cabinet during the Cuban Missile Crisis, 1962.

THE PRESIDENT AT WORK IN THE OVAL OFFICE

President Lyndon B. Johnson talks on the phone in the Oval Office while watching the news on three television sets. He also monitored world events on the wire service ticker tapes (installed to the left of the televisions).

President Richard Nixon meets with Israeli Prime Minister Golda Meir and Henry Kissinger in the Oval Office, 1973.

Left: President George H. W. Bush meets with advisers in the Oval Office during the first hours of the Gulf War, January 18, 1991.

Below left: President Bill Clinton reading in the Oval Office, 1995.

Below right: President George W. Bush signs the supplemental bill for relief aid following Hurricane Katrina, 2005.

President Jimmy Carter
with Vice President
Walter Mondale during
the Iran Hostage Crisis,
January 1981.

irrevocable decision to block Soviet ships
from bringing more ballistic missiles to
Cuba. Until the Soviet Union backed off,
the world's future wavered in the balance.
During the late 1960s, the riots in
American cities and the escalation of the
Vietnam War with the deaths of American
soldiers weighed heavily on Lyndon B.
Johnson, who chose not to run for
reelection in 1968.

Five years later, an unprecedented
domestic crisis cast its first dark shadow
across the Nixon White House with news
of a break-in at the offices of the
Democratic National Committee in the
capital. The seemingly minor incident
grew into a series of investigations and
criminal indictments that resulted in
intense pressure on Nixon to resign in

the face of almost certain impeachment.
Gerald Ford endured much criticism for
his pardon of Nixon and faced challenges
related to the economy. Jimmy Carter had
to deal with a national energy shortage
and the seizure of U.S. embassy staff in
Iran. Ronald Reagan was confronted with
the bombing of a Marine barracks in
Beirut; his dramatic meetings with Soviet
President Mikhail Gorbachev produced a
treaty signed in the East Room to limit
certain nuclear missiles. The cold war
ended following the fall of the Berlin wall
during George H. W. Bush's tenure, but
other areas demanded his attention. He
sent American troops into Panama when
the security of the Panama Canal was
threatened, and into the Middle East when
Iraq invaded Kuwait. William J. Clinton

sent American forces to Somalia and Bosnia. Then, less than a year after his inauguration, George W. Bush responded to terrorist attacks by sending American troops into Afghanistan and, in 2003, to war in Iraq.

As the representative of all the people, the president must balance the often-conflicting interests of many groups and sections in seeking the common good. Yet he can never forget that the individual American also looks directly to him as the holder of the office that—in Herbert Hoover's words—"touches the happiness of every home."

Seldom, if ever, can the chief executive escape the pressures of his job, whether engaging in a favorite sport or relaxing in the intimacy of his family circle. To all,

friends or strangers, he has suddenly become a man whose magic words can unlock the gifts of position and wealth. His election has given him powers that in scope and variety are unique. He is at once the ceremonial head of government, leader of a political party, administrator of the nation's laws and domestic affairs, director of foreign policy, and commander in chief of the armed forces. How this many-faceted power has been used has depended on the era, the character, and the conscience of each president, for the Constitution offers few specific guidelines for the conduct of the office. As Woodrow Wilson put it, the president is "at liberty . . . to be as big a man as he can. His capacity will set the limit."

President Ronald Reagan and Soviet President Mikhail Gorbachev sign the Intermediate Range Nuclear Forces (INF) Treaty in the East Room, 1987.

Where Hospitality Makes History

2

Whatever their personal style, no president and his wife can ever forget that they act as the nation's official host and hostess. The distinctive architecture of the Executive Residence, with its spacious rooms and elegant parlors, lends itself to both casual and formal gatherings. Though each administration leaves its own distinctive social imprint on White House entertaining, the hospitality always retains its symbolic meaning in the house that belongs to all Americans.

Diana, Princess of Wales, dances with actor John Travolta at a White House dinner during the Reagan administration, 1985.

EARLY TRADITIONS IN WHITE HOUSE ENTERTAINING

Recognizing their responsibility for setting national standards of hospitality, John and Abigail Adams required guests to show the kind of deference to the new republic that subjects accorded rulers of monarchies abroad. During their short stay in the village capital, the Adamses practiced the formal court etiquette that had been adopted for a similar reason by George and Martha Washington in New York and Philadelphia. Mrs. Adams remained regally seated to greet the town's leading citizens and foreign diplomats who attended the president's levees, or receptions. By her side, dressed in a black velvet coat, John Adams bowed solemnly to arrivals, who then took designated seats around the wall.

Such formality went out the window when Thomas Jefferson became president.

This modern watercolor depicts a reception during the presidency of John Adams. Visitors entered the Oval Room (known today as the Blue Room) from a temporary wooden balcony on the south side of the house. The South Portico was not added until 1824.

He emphasized, instead, his cherished ideals of equality and democracy. In his words, he "buried . . . levees, birthdays, royal parades" and replaced them with two main White House receptions, which were open to all, on New Year's Day and the Fourth of July.

Jefferson entertained Jérôme Bonaparte, Napoleon's youngest brother and the future king of Westphalia, after that impetuous young man married the Baltimore belle, Betsy Patterson. Jefferson once invited his butcher to dinner. The man brought his son, explaining that the boy could use the place vacated by a guest who was ill. And the president made both feel welcome among the distinguished company. Jefferson's dislike for ceremony, however, only highlighted his refined taste. He served fine wines and hired a French chef to prepare the foods unfamiliar to Americans. Around his small, informal table, he assembled the wittiest, most knowledgeable men and women to be found in the city or coming from abroad to visit the strange young capital.

In learning and accomplishments, Jefferson himself was unique. His interests ranged from music and history to farming, astronomy, anthropology, and architecture. And it was this erudition that President John F. Kennedy referred to in his famous toast at a 1962 dinner honoring Nobel Prize winners. His guests, said Kennedy, made up "the most extraordinary collection of talent, of human knowledge, that has ever been gathered together at the White House, with the possible exception of when Thomas Jefferson dined alone."

Jefferson replaced the custom of bowing with the more democratic practice of shaking hands. The greeting proved so popular that no successor could abandon

President Andrew Johnson receives callers at a New Year's reception in 1866.

it, despite the painful pressure from thousands of hands embracing the privilege. Slight James K. Polk, once described as the "merest tangible fraction of a president," found a way to avoid a painful grip. "When I observed a strong man approaching," he said, "I generally took advantage of him by being a little quicker . . . seizing him by the top of his fingers, giving him a hearty shake."

Abraham Lincoln performed the task, in the words of an observer, "as though . . . splitting rails as of yore." On January 1, 1863, before signing the Emancipation Proclamation, he shook hands for three hours at the usual New Year's reception. Upstairs in his Cabinet Room, he spread the official document on the table, dipped

Visitors wait in line along the North Drive to attend a New Year's reception hosted by President Theodore Roosevelt in 1903.

his pen in ink, and paused. "I never . . . felt more certain that I was doing right," he said, looking at Secretary of State William H. Seward. "But . . . my arm is stiff and numb . . . if they find my hand trembled, they will say, 'he had some compunctions.' But, any way, it is going to be done!" Then, slowly and carefully, Lincoln wrote the bold signature that appears at the end of the document.

Besides shaking hands with the public at special events, most presidents regularly made themselves available for the ritual as recently as the time of Calvin Coolidge. White House doors were then opened for the purpose weekly. Rather surprisingly, the taciturn New Englander thoroughly enjoyed the contact.

"On one occasion I shook hands with nineteen hundred in thirty-four minutes," Coolidge recalled in his autobiography. "Instead of a burden, it was a pleasure and a relief to meet people in that way and listen to their greeting, which was often a benediction."

When Herbert Hoover and his wife, Lou, opened the White House for a traditional New Year's Day reception in 1930, six thousand people appeared. By 1932, the annual open house and handshaking had become such an ordeal that the Hoovers decided to be out of town the following year. The custom was never revived.

No one ever took more delight in receiving people and making them welcome

Visitors form a line along the North Drive to shake hands with President Calvin Coolidge at the New Year's reception in 1927.

than did vivacious Dolley Madison. Even before she became first lady, she sometimes served as official hostess for the widowed Jefferson while her husband James Madison was secretary of state. After she moved into the mansion in 1809, Dolley made the President's House the rallying point of Washington's fast-burgeoning social life. In the "blazing splendor" of her drawing room, as Washington Irving described it, were gathered, said another guest, "all these whom fashion, fame, beauty, wealth or talents, have render'd celebrated."

While "the great little Madison" met with his cabinet, Dolley often entertained the wives at "dove parties." Taking no sides in political disputes of the day, she was cordial to Federalist and Republican leaders alike. To callers in general, she served refreshments of seedcake and hot bouillon in winter, punch in summer. Perhaps compensating for the subdued dress of her Quaker girlhood, Dolley Madison arrayed herself in rich silks and satins and accentuated her height with magnificent turbans, sometimes decked with ostrich plumes. Yet so obvious was her honest friendliness that everyone found her appealing, notwithstanding her exaggerated dress and mannerisms. "'Tis here the woman who adorns the dress," said a contemporary commentator; "in her hands the snuffbox seems only a gracious implement."

Then suddenly, brutally, the mansion's "Golden Age," as some called the Madison era of entertaining, came to an end. The War of 1812 had broken out five months before Madison's reelection. It dragged on, mostly in sea engagements far from Washington, until the electrifying news struck the capital on a hot August 23, 1814, that the British had landed troops in Maryland. Gathering members of his cabinet, President Madison went off early the next day to join the American forces near Bladensburg, Maryland. Meantime, Mrs. Madison remained at the White House, overseeing a dinner for the president and watching through a spyglass for her husband to return, "ready at a moment's warning to enter my carriage and leave the city," as she wrote her sister in an hour-by-hour letter. "I am still here within sound of the cannon!" she added at 3:00 in the afternoon. "Two messengers covered with dust, come to bid me fly; but I wait for him." Friends finally persuaded Dolley to leave and escorted her across the Potomac into Virginia, where she eventually would join the president. Her flight came none too soon. Having scattered the Bladensburg defenders, the British troops marched into Washington that evening and put the torch to the White House, the Capitol, and other public buildings. A torrential thunderstorm saved the city from devastating destruction, but the Executive Mansion was reduced to a blackened, burned-out shell.

Reconstruction took three years. During the remainder of Madison's administration, the couple lived in rented houses, where the incomparable Dolley held court

The White House is seen engulfed in flames on the night of August 24, 1814, during the War of 1812, in this watercolor painted in 2004. The blaze, set by British troops who hurled flaming torches through the windows, gutted the interior and was finally extinguished by a raging thunderstorm.

Tom Freeman
© 2004

The exterior walls were all that remained of the White House after the fire of 1814. The burned, soot-covered shell is seen in this watercolor by George Munger, c. 1814–15.

and the president conducted executive affairs in an atmosphere of renewed confidence following the country's second confrontation with the British.

When James Monroe and his family moved into the rebuilt White House in the fall of 1817, its partially rebuilt exterior had again been painted a gleaming white. Handsomely restored inside, it contained elegantly carved and gilded furniture and decorative objects in the State Rooms, many of them ordered by Monroe from France. Nor were the appearances deceptive. The new facade and furnishings marked a return to the pomp of earlier days.

Guests at the first New Year's reception had a preview of the changed rules

when foreign diplomats were greeted with elaborate protocol before the public was admitted. From then on, Monroe insisted, as had Washington and Adams, that respect be shown the United States by placing foreign ministers "upon much the same footing . . . of form and ceremony" as that required of American ministers at European courts. This meant that diplomats would come to the White House only by invitation or after requesting a formal audience with the president.

First Lady Elizabeth Monroe adopted a chillier social tone. She refused to continue the exhausting custom of making first calls to cabinet wives or women in the city, or even returning them. Eliza Hay, the Monroes' married daughter who lived in the White House with her husband, carried on her own feud with Diplomatic Corps wives over the etiquette of paying calls. The drastic change from the Madisons' warmth and accessibility alienated Washington's social leaders. They retaliated by boycotting the Monroes' "at homes." "The drawing room of the President was opened last night to a 'beggarly row of empty chairs,'" wrote Mrs. William Winston Seaton, wife of a prominent Washington newspaper editor. "Only five females attended, three of whom were foreigners."

In long-range social prestige, however, the White House always wins. Washington society eventually accepted the Monroes' rules of etiquette, along with their hospitality. Moreover, future first ladies would be forever indebted to Elizabeth Monroe for freeing them from the demands of local sociabilities.

The Monroes' successors, John Quincy Adams and his wife, continued the high style of entertaining, bringing to it a background of the longest and most varied diplomatic and social experience abroad that any president has ever had. John Quincy, son of the first president to live in the White House, had served in United States missions at many courts, including Prussia, the Netherlands, and England. His wife, Louisa Johnson Adams, born in London to an American father and an English mother, was a brilliant scholar and an accomplished hostess. Well read in Greek, French, and English literature, she wrote verse in French, played the harp and spinet, and maintained her equanimity

under the heavy pressure of official entertaining.

"This evening was the sixth drawing-room," President Adams wrote in his diary after one of the public levees that were held every fortnight. "Very much crowded; sixteen Senators, perhaps sixty members of the House of Representatives, and multitudes of strangers . . . these parties are becoming more and more insupportable."

As a conscientious New Englander, however, Adams never shirked his duty. He met punctiliously with his guests and served even more elaborate refreshments than had his predecessor. The loaded trays carried by waiters threading their way through crowded State Rooms held ice cream, coffee, tea, cakes, jellies, wines, and liqueurs — plus various imported West Indian fruits in season.

Perhaps the most notable dinner presided over by John Quincy Adams was one in 1825 honoring the Marquis de Lafayette on his sixty-eighth birthday. The French hero of the Revolutionary War, who was paying a return visit to America, responded thus to the president's toasts to his and George Washington's birthdays: "To the Fourth of July," he said, "the birthday of liberty in both continents."

John Quincy Adams ended his one-term presidency in deep chagrin over his defeat by the West's magnetic general, Andrew Jackson. He did not linger to attend the inaugural ceremonies, which culminated in the most boisterous celebration ever seen at the White House.

President Andrew Jackson invited the public to feast on a 1,400 pound cheese, which was placed in the Entrance Hall in February 1837. Jackson had been given the cheese in celebration of George Washington's birthday.

The enthusiastic followers of the veteran Indian fighter and hero of the battle of New Orleans poured into Washington from far and near to see the "People's President" installed in the highest post of the land. Frontiersmen, clerks, and bankers, some with wives and children, jammed the boardinghouses and hotels. "It was like the inundation of the northern barbarians into Rome," said one eyewitness.

After applauding Jackson's inaugural address at the Capitol, the crowd moved on to enjoy the White House reception—to the accompaniment of crashing china and glassware. Attendants lured many of the unruly guests out to the lawn for punch served from buckets. Inside, merrymakers stood in muddy boots on satin upholstered chairs to catch a glimpse of their new leader, while would-be handshakers backed him against the wall. The president escaped the mob's further embrace only by slipping out and spending the night at the "Wigwam," as capital residents had nicknamed the nearby Gadsby's Hotel. Yet the rude opening of the Jackson administration was far from an accurate foretaste of "Old Hickory's" tenure in the White House.

At his official receptions and suppers, Jackson also offered guests sumptuous repasts, including the best wines and liqueurs, and every kind of meat and fowl the lush new land afforded. The last open house held by Jackson was almost as crowded as his first. On the eve of leaving office in 1837, he was presented with a 1,400-pound cheese. Placing the huge gift in the Entrance Hall, he invited the public to come and eat as much as they liked in celebration of George Washington's birthday. The people came in droves. What they did not eat dropped on the floor and was trod into the carpets; the smell lingered for weeks.

The whole affair, some said, effectively discouraged public entertaining by incoming President Martin Van Buren, who was Jackson's vice president and his handpicked choice for the nation's top office. Whatever his reason, Van Buren—a widower for years—discontinued all public receptions except those on New Year's Day and the Fourth of July. Instead of the openhanded hospitality of the Jackson era,

A BEAUTIFUL GOBLET OF WHITE·HOUSE CHAMPAGNE

he arranged small, exclusive dinner parties, where both friendly and opposing political leaders traded lively repartee.

The president's four bachelor sons, who lived with him and shared his social and political interests, presented an irresistible challenge to Washington matchmakers. Dolley Madison—by now an aging but still romantic widow—won the

Pictured holding a glass of champagne and living in high style, President Martin Van Buren was caricatured by his opponent during the presidential campaign of 1840.

The White House collection contains this campaign textile from the presidential election of 1840, which pictures a log cabin and a barrel of hard cider, symbols for successful candidate William Henry Harrison, pictured at the bottom.

$3,665 for the mansion's maintenance. In what would become famous as the "Gold Spoon Oration," Ogle described Van Buren as one who used "knives, forks, and spoons of gold that he may dine in the style of the monarchs of Europe." He spent "the People's cash in . . . green finger cups, in which to wash his pretty tapering, soft, white lily fingers," and ate fancy French foods instead of good American "'hog and hominy,' 'fried meat and gravy' . . . with a mug of 'hard cider.'" Van Buren's defenders assembled figures to prove that their man actually was costing the taxpayers less for house expenses than had any other president. But the gold-spoon image had been created, and in 1840 the voters elected the president's opponent, William Henry Harrison, candidate of the Whig "Log Cabin and Hard Cider" Party.

Harrison's wife, Anna, was the only first lady who never acted in her official role. She did not even see the White House. At the time of the inauguration she was unable to stand the rough coach-and-steamer trip from her home on the Ohio frontier. She was about to leave when a messenger rode up with news of the president's death one month after his inauguration. It was too late to attend the state funeral for her husband. She remained in Ohio, where Harrison had made his career —and where their grandson, Benjamin Harrison, would start on his path to the presidency nearly half a century later.

Thus the White House received an unexpected resident in John Tyler, who as the vice presidential candidate had been

prize by introducing Van Buren's eldest son, Abraham, to Angelica Singleton, a lovely young relative of hers then visiting the capital from South Carolina. As Mrs. Abraham Van Buren, charming Angelica made a perfect hostess for her father-in-law. But the president's enemies found a rich lode of political capital in what they pictured as selfish high living in the Executive Mansion while the country suffered from a severe depression. Congressman Charles Ogle of Pennsylvania led the attack in blocking an appropriation of the last half of Harrison's catchy campaign slogan, "Tippecanoe and Tyler Too." President Tyler, labeled "His Accidency" by unkind critics, was destined to remain in the mansion only a single term. But he brought to it in turn two wives as different as they could be. Gentle Letitia, his first wife and mother of eight children, led the retiring life of an invalid until her death in 1842. Acting in her stead, her daughter-in-law, Priscilla (married to son Robert), performed as a highly successful official hostess on such glittering occasions as the State Dinner and ball given for the Prince de Joinville, son of Louis Philippe of France.

Tyler's second wife, lighthearted 24-year-old Julia Gardiner—a belle at home and abroad before her marriage—frankly enjoyed the attention she received as the nation's first lady. Seated in a large armchair on a platform in the Blue Room, the erstwhile "Rose of Long Island" greeted guests with the air of a queen. In a white satin ball gown and gleaming headdress adorned with diamonds and ostrich feathers, she led the dancing in the East Room as gentlemen whirled their partners in the then-daring waltz. At one reception she introduced a bouncy Bohemian dance called the polka and started it toward wide popularity. After an especially triumphant evening, Julia Tyler wrote her mother with girlish delight, "The British Minister, Pakenham, was there . . . and devoted to me. At least fifty members of Congress paid their respects to me, and all at one time."

To pleasure-loving members of the capital's higher echelons, the dancing steps of the second Mrs. Tyler gave way far too quickly to the dogged tread of all-work-and-no-play President James K. Polk and his attractive but straitlaced Sarah, a devout Presbyterian. New rules banned dancing, card playing, and similar diversions. The proper Polks did their duty, offering the required number of formal dinners and grand receptions, but no food or beverages refreshed the great dry public gatherings, which were famous for sedateness and sobriety. A guest who ventured to compliment the first lady on the "genteel assemblage" at one of these receptions received Sarah Polk's dignified reply: "Sir, I have never seen it otherwise."

The next three presidents—Zachary Taylor, Millard Fillmore, and Franklin Pierce—had little chance to enliven the

This early daguerreotype captures President and Mrs. James K. Polk with their guests at the White House in 1849. From left to right: future president James Buchanan; Harriet Lane (Buchanan's niece); Joanna Rucker (Mrs. Polk's niece); postmaster general Cave Johnson; Mrs. Polk; Secretary of the Treasury Robert Walker; President Polk; former First Lady Dolley Madison; and Matilda Childress Polk (Mrs. Polk's cousin).

Edward, Prince of Wales, visited President James Buchanan in 1860. He is seen here receiving guests in the East Room.

Washington social scene. The popular former general, "Old Rough and Ready" Taylor, died after only sixteen months in office. During that time his delicate wife, Margaret, had relied on their married daughter, Betty Bliss, to do the honors at official functions.

Ailing Abigail Fillmore also was forced to delegate many of her hostess chores to her daughter, Mary Abigail. Yet, as the president's wife, she managed to put in an appearance and to greet guests at a surprising number of dinners and receptions in spite of delicate health and the pain that came from standing on a permanently injured ankle.

One of the gloomiest periods in White House entertaining prevailed during the

Pierce administration, which began two months after the Pierces had witnessed the death of their last surviving child, Benjamin, killed in a railroad accident. Naturally limited at first, White House social functions continued thereafter in a stiff and somber atmosphere, which extended even to Jane Pierce's large table bouquets of rigidly wired japonicas.

The return of what a reporter called "joy and gladness in the Executive Mansion" came, ironically enough, in the ominous pre–Civil War term of James Buchanan. One cause for joy was Buchanan's beautiful young niece and ward, Harriet Lane. As his official hostess, she presided over so many brilliant balls and sumptuous banquets that

the White House was compared to a European court.

The Buchanan White House frequently drew titled travelers. Journalists wrote about the first diplomatic mission to Washington from Imperial Japan in the spring of 1860. Delivering a commercial treaty, the sixty-member entourage created a sensation in the mansion's East Room, where curious Americans viewed the envoys' exotic clothing and hairstyles. As a final social coup in his politically weak administration, President Buchanan welcomed the Prince of Wales, later Britain's Edward VII, as a houseguest. Miss Lane arranged a State Dinner with royal protocol, followed by fireworks on the lawn. But the public reception for the prince

turned into a roughhouse. "The Royal party have certainly seen Democracy unshackled for once," wrote a New York correspondent. "The rush . . . was terrible. People clambered in and jumped out of the windows."

During the Civil War, White House entertaining took a new direction. The Union capital was crowded with Union army and navy officers, war contractors, and assorted visitors who came to see President Lincoln and to share the first family's hospitality. Special dinners and receptions were given for high government officials, staff officers, and diplomats. To the weekly public levees came crowds of soldiers and day laborers along with the most fashionable ladies and

The first envoys from Imperial Japan pay their respects to President James Buchanan and his cabinet during an East Room reception in 1860.

gentlemen. Attired "with gloves and without gloves; clean and dirty," they all pressed toward "the tall, rapidly bobbing head of the good 'Abe,' as he shook hands with his guests," recalled one bystander; and "when anyone he knew came along, he bent himself down to the necessary level, and seemed to whisper a few words in the ear, in pleasant, homely fashion."

First Lady Mary Lincoln held afternoon receptions, too, and carefully planned major social events. But nothing she did could please her relentless critics. If she served fine food, the first lady was wasting money while brave boys died at the front. If she held only a reception instead of a formal dinner, her critics said she must have been saving money for the personal finery that everyone knew to be her weakness. Yet the same public committed shocking acts of vandalism in the president's home. Guests at Lincoln's second inaugural reception cut souvenirs of floral designs from brocaded window draperies and lace curtains; damage was extensive. After Lincoln's assassination, ruthless collectors ravaged the house. "Silver and dining ware were carried off," wrote an eyewitness. "It was plundered not only of ornaments but of heavy articles of furniture. Costly sofas and chairs were cut and injured."

President Abraham Lincoln is depicted welcoming guests to a "Grand Reception" at the White House in 1862.

White House Hospitality in the Victorian Era

Following the Civil War, White House hospitality continued to reflect the attitudes of each new set of residents as they adapted themselves and their house to changing times. When Andrew Johnson and his family moved into the shabby building in the summer of 1865, they brought to its renovation a sturdy common sense that might well have served as an example to politicians during the turbulent days of Reconstruction.

"We are plain people from the mountains of Tennessee," said the Johnsons' older daughter, Martha Patterson, who directed most of the work and took over as official hostess for her invalid mother. "I trust too much will not be expected of us," she added, and then proceeded to extend the family's hospitality with natural good

King David Kalakaua of the Hawaiian Islands, the first head of state to visit the White House, greets President Ulysses S. Grant at a reception in December 1874.

taste and a charm that surprised and won over many Washington sophisticates. The Johnsons also showed how "plain people" could stand with dignity during the terrible weeks before the president's impeachment trial ended in his vindication. But it was a miserable time for all.

The inauguration of popular Union general Ulysses S. Grant on March 4, 1869, finally opened the floodgates for long-deferred capital celebrations. Julia Grant relished her role as mistress of the White House. She found it, she wrote, "a garden spot of orchids . . . a constant feast of cleverness and wit, with men who were the brainiest . . . and women unrivalled for beauty, talent and tact."

The Grants entertained often and lavishly. In 1874 King David Kalakaua of the Sandwich Islands—now Hawaii—became the first ruling monarch to visit the White House. At a State Dinner in his honor, three of the king's retinue stood behind him, and one examined each dish before his master accepted it.

If the Grant administration typified mid-Victorian style in multiple table courses and intricate decor, President and Mrs. Rutherford B. Hayes followed as perfect examples of the era's ideal of moral rectitude. Few White House scenes were ever more sedate than the Sunday-evening hymn sings and prayers that congressional and cabinet friends shared with the presidential family. After an April 1877 dinner for Grand Duke Alexis, son of the Russian czar, no alcoholic beverage, including wine, was served at White House func-

tions—a prohibition that later earned Mrs. Hayes the nickname of "Lemonade Lucy" and brought a quip from one guest that "water flowed like wine."

The more relaxed yet intellectual social atmosphere that marked the beginning of James A. Garfield's term as the next president is often obscured by the tragedy of his assassination. Both he and his wife, Lucretia, were warm, cultured people. A classical scholar, Garfield sometimes performed the trick of simultaneously writing Greek with one hand and Latin with the other. Mrs. Garfield was perhaps the first first lady to initiate serious research on White House history. Then, without warning, the bright four-month tenure of the Garfields ended on July 2, 1881, with shots fired by a demented office seeker. Garfield died two months later.

The new chief executive, former Vice President Chester Arthur, was a debonair widower who became the most eligible catch in town. His huge wardrobe and handsome carriage with his coat-of-arms on the door were topics of conversation, his elegant dinners the most sought after. Mary Arthur McElroy, his youngest sister, came from her home in Albany, New York, to assist him as hostess.

The people's next choice was America's second bachelor president, Grover Cleveland, who soon chose as his bride his young ward Frances Folsom. As a hostess, she proved as capable as she was beautiful. She organized functions well in advance and showed her stamina by shaking hands

Above: President and Mrs. Grover Cleveland welcome guests at an Army Navy reception held in 1888.

Opposite: First Lady Lucy Webb Hayes greets her guests in the Blue Room in 1877.

with an estimated nine thousand guests at one public reception. She arranged at-home days so that all women who wished to meet her could. She held two receptions a week, one on Saturdays so that working women could attend. Indeed, energetic Mrs. Cleveland so enjoyed life in the White House that she left tearfully in 1889, remarking to a member of the house staff that she and her husband would be back. Four years later she kept her promise. Cleveland was reelected and became the only president to serve non-consecutive terms.

The Victorian Age gave us two more first ladies, each representative of the period in her own way. Caroline Scott Harrison, wife of Benjamin Harrison, brought to her new role the same energy she had shown in church and club work back in Ohio. A model of domesticity, she presided over the White House with genteel efficiency. She assembled pieces of White House china used by previous families, thus beginning the preservation of the historic White House china collection.

President William McKinley's wife, Ida, embodied a no less typically Victorian image of the delicate female. Though in poor health, she made valiant efforts to cope with official schedules. She attended exhausting State Dinners, at which the usual seating arrangement was changed to place her beside her devoted husband, who could thus see to her needs. From a chair near the receiving line at receptions, Ida greeted guests but held a bouquet to foil handshakers.

Entertaining in the Twentieth Century

As the twentieth century arrived, it was no coincidence that the dynamic character and deeds of Theodore Roosevelt reflected America's exuberance, growing power, and influence. By moving his offices to the new West Wing and remodeling the mansion's State Rooms after the simple elegance of the early nineteenth century, the president at once gained quarters for increasing executive business and created a more appropriate setting for the nation's official entertaining.

From December 1902, when the renovation was completed, social functions began to take on the more regulated character of modern times. The Roosevelts employed the first White House social secretary, and the president delegated a government official to untangle sticky

President Theodore Roosevelt prepares to toast the guest of honor Prince Henry of Prussia at a dinner in the East Room, 1902.

problems of precedence involving diplomatic and political rivalries.

Roosevelt imparted his own ebullience to every White House event—from a reunion with the Rough Riders of the Spanish-American War to a Japanese jujitsu exhibition in the East Room, or to formal state functions, such as the reception and spectacular stag dinner for Prince Henry of Prussia. Roosevelt also made history with his 1901 dinner invitation to Booker T. Washington, the first African American to receive a social invitation to the President's House. TR's charming wife, Edith, brought to her official duties a poise that led the president's military aide, Archie Butt, to write that she spent seven years as first lady "without ever having made a mistake."

The last century of social history at the White House has clearly shown how life in the Executive Residence is colored by each family's personality and background.

President and Mrs. William Howard Taft were the first to entertain on the roof of the terrace leading to the new west extension, where they sat at wicker tables under Chinese lanterns swaying in the breeze. The social highlight of their White House years was the celebration of their twenty-fifth wedding anniversary on June 19, 1911, when they gave a large evening garden party on the South Lawn for several thousand people.

Woodrow Wilson, who like John Tyler became a widower while in office and who also brought a second wife to the mansion, had firm ideas of his role as

President William Howard Taft greets society during a White House reception, 1911.

host. Regardless of pressures, he refused to invite anyone to the White House to advance even the most precious of his programs. "I will not permit my home to be used for political purposes," Wilson declared. And although he presided with good humor at official parties, he preferred small dinners in the Jeffersonian manner—animated by witty and intellectual conversation. Wilson found with his second wife, Edith, a renewal of happiness he had never expected to know again. Without her "love and care . . . I don't believe he could live," Mrs. Wilson's social secretary, Edith Benham, wrote in the dark days after the strain of his stubborn but futile League of Nations campaign had left him a paralyzed, broken man.

President Warren G. Harding poses with visiting American Indians, c. 1921–23.

After the grim days of World War I and the gloom of Wilson's long illness, the arrival of genial Warren G. Harding seemed to bring back the pleasant days of "normalcy" he had promised. Not only did the new president and his wife, Florence, reopen the doors for large and frequent official gatherings, but they also dined almost daily with Harding's card-playing cronies and other close friends. They opened the mansion to public tours once again after it had been closed during World War I; on such occasions, Mrs. Harding sometimes appeared unexpectedly and shook hands with astonished, delighted sightseers. Though she suffered from a chronic kidney ailment, she energetically went about her duties as

first lady. Then, suddenly, following the president's death during a trip to the West in 1923, the convivial period ended.

To the Executive Mansion came the rock-ribbed New Englander and former vice president, Calvin Coolidge, and his charming wife, Grace. Social life during the Coolidge administration was notable for the many anecdotes it produced concerning the granite reserve and wry humor of the president. The early morning breakfasts to which Coolidge invited members of Congress — often to the dismay of late sleepers — gave capital raconteurs some of their best stories. One told of the time the president poured coffee and cream into his saucer. As a few guests followed suit, Coolidge

President and Mrs. Calvin Coolidge pose with military and naval aides who assisted in the New Year's reception, January 1, 1927.

calmly put the saucer on the floor for his dog.

The most famous guest of the time, loquacious Queen Marie of Romania, was entertained at a State Dinner in 1926. According to Chief Usher Ike Hoover, the queen made strenuous efforts to get "Silent Cal" to talk, but "was not any more successful than others who had tried it before." The whole affair was odd, the chief usher noted, for the visit, including ceremonial greetings, the meal, and farewells, took only an hour and forty-five minutes.

Yet, in the matter of etiquette, President Coolidge inaugurated what has become an indispensable aid in conducting state visits. Following an awkward incident in which wartime enemies were seated together at an official dinner, he established a Protocol Office in the State Department to handle procedures for such visits. Today its staff arranges programs, determines precedence, and suggests food preferences to fit the specific needs of each delegation.

White House entertaining reached new heights when President Herbert Hoover assumed office amid a seemingly endless boom economy. Even after the stock market crashed in the autumn of 1929, the wealthy president and his wife, Lou, continued to invite a record number of guests for breakfast, lunch, and dinner, though they personally met the expenses not only for their private parties but also for many of the official ones.

President Herbert Hoover presents aviator Amelia Earhart with a gold medal for her trans-Atlantic flight, 1932.

No one could assume, however, that such hospitality marked indifference to the nation's problems. The Quaker president had long shown his humanity in war and postwar relief work in food distribution, and he labored to solve the country's gargantuan economic troubles. At times he would gulp his meals so fast, a member of the domestic staff recalled, that "the servants made bets on how long it would take . . . 'nine minutes, fifteen seconds,' or whatever."

Franklin Delano Roosevelt and his big, gregarious clan came next, to meet the challenge of the Depression and usher in the longest, most varied social period yet. Eleanor Roosevelt in her book *This I Remember* listed a staggering number of

official and personal luncheons, teas, dinners, receptions, and other programs. In one year alone, President and Mrs. Roosevelt put up 323 houseguests, served meals to 4,729 people, and offered refreshments at teas and receptions to 14,056 others. The assorted guests pouring into and out of the mansion between March 1933 and April 1945 included students, poets, playwrights, labor leaders, nuclear scientists, prime ministers, and presidents. During World War II, British Prime Minister Winston Churchill came often and stayed in the White House, and the mysterious visitor of 1942, known only as Mr. Brown, turned out to be Soviet Foreign Minister V. M. Molotov on a mission to speed up

Above: President Franklin D. Roosevelt and Winston Churchill during a May 1943 meeting at the White House.

Left: First Lady Eleanor Roosevelt with guests at a lawn party honoring U.S. soldiers in 1942.

the opening of an Allied second front in Europe.

World War II gave a regal dimension to the Roosevelts' hospitality with the appearance of royal refugees fleeing Nazi occupation in Europe. Some, such as the Crown Prince and Princess of Norway and Queen Wilhelmina of the Netherlands, became temporary houseguests. Others, such as the kings of Greece and Yugoslavia, were briefly feted. Older Washingtonians recall the White House visit of Britain's King George VI and Queen Elizabeth just before war erupted in 1939. Down the hall from the family rooms on the Second Floor, the king occupied the Lincoln suite, his queen, the Rose suite, later called the Queens' Bedroom. Screens separated the royal and presidential quarters.

By the time of President Harry S. Truman and his wife, Bess, the "season" had expanded to include half a dozen State Dinners and as many congressional and other large receptions. Some were so well attended that guests stood almost shoulder-to-shoulder. At a reception in 1948, the chandelier in the Blue Room tinkled a warning that the structure was in critically shaky condition. During the following three and one-half years, while the White House underwent reconstruction, the Trumans lived across the street in the government's guest residence, Blair House, and large official dinners and receptions took place in local hotels. In 1951 Britain's Princess Elizabeth and her husband, Philip, Duke of Edinburgh, spent several days at Blair House with the Trumans.

The next year, the presidential family moved back into the restored Executive Mansion just in time to welcome as houseguests Queen Juliana of the Netherlands and her consort, Prince Bernhard. But capital life was changing in the postwar era. State visitors came so frequently from newly independent nations and as a result of foreign policy conferences and fast modern transport that the White House could no longer accommodate them.

Since the latter part of the Eisenhower administration, most official guests have stayed at Blair House, across Pennsylvania Avenue from the White House, during their state visits. In fact, only once during Dwight Eisenhower's second term did guests sleep in the mansion—when Elizabeth II, queen of Great Britain, and Prince

The arrival of Prime Minister Ali Liaquat Khan of Pakistan at Blair House in 1950. The residence on Pennsylvania Avenue was used by the Trumans during the three and one-half year renovation of the White House.

President and Mrs. Dwight D. Eisenhower greet Great Britain's Queen Elizabeth II and Prince Philip at the North Portico on their arrival for a four-day stay in October 1957.

Grand Duchess Charlotte of Luxembourg and First Lady Jacqueline Kennedy compliment actor Basil Rathbone and members of the consort players who had presented an evening of Elizabethan poetry and music in the East Room, April 1963.

Philip occupied the same suites as had her mother and father nearly twenty years before. President and Mrs. Eisenhower enjoyed the formal ceremonial role of official entertaining that reflected their years of military life.

Under the lively direction of John F. and Jacqueline Kennedy in the early 1960s, official entertaining changed further. President Kennedy banished receiving lines whenever possible and chatted informally with guests in the connecting State Rooms. At round tables, rather than the more formal U-shaped ones, shorter dinners with fewer courses, prepared by a French chef, allowed the guests more time to dance and to watch performances of internationally known musicians, ballet dancers, opera singers, jazz stars, and Shakespearean actors.

Then came the crack of rifle shots in Dallas — and a black interlude of international mourning for the bright, lost promise of a murdered president. When social life returned to the White House, the new host brought with him a quarter century of capital friendships and service, first as representative and senator from Texas, then as vice president. It was not surprising that an atmosphere of Texas Americana pervaded the private and official parties of Lyndon B. Johnson and his wife, Claudia, better known by her childhood nickname, "Lady Bird."

In January 1969 the spotlight on executive entertaining moved from the

Above: President and Mrs.
Richard Nixon pose with
guests the Duke and
Duchess of Windsor at a
White House dinner, 1970.

Left: President and Mrs.
Gerald R. Ford listen to an
impromptu performance by
legendary bandleader
Harry James, June 1975.

President and Mrs. Jimmy Carter frequently entertained outdoors. In June 1978 they held a jazz festival on the South Lawn featuring Eubie Blake performing ragtime.

Johnsons to the Nixons, another family with two daughters. But the resemblance ended there, for Richard and Pat Nixon, like those who went before, soon produced an entertainment pattern all their own. One innovation was a series of Sunday morning worship services attended by associates and friends of the family. Held in the East Room and presided over by leaders of various faiths, the services were followed by a social hour and refreshments in the State Dining Room. As events unfolded over the next years, the Nixon administration ended in political scandals and the president's resignation—and a new family in the old house.

From August 1974 to January 1977 the Gerald Fords made their own brand of

White House history. Guests remembered lively dinners capped by dancing in the Entrance Hall, where Betty Ford, who once studied modern dance with the noted Martha Graham Dance Company of New York, whirled gracefully with the president and other partners. During the nation's Bicentennial celebrations in 1976, the Fords hosted numerous heads of state and held many events in the White House to commemorate the country's history.

With the Georgia Carters, still another regional design went into the tapestry of White House hospitality, which never ceases to repeat the infinite variety of American life. "Natural," "spontaneous," and "family oriented" were terms often used by the media to describe Jimmy and

Rosalynn's southern style. Their creative entertaining was enhanced by the world-famous American and European performers they introduced in the East Room. On a memorable evening following the ceremonial signing of the Panama Canal treaties, the Carters' dinner guests included eighteen heads of Latin American states and twenty-five U.S. senators.

Ronald and Nancy Reagan also hosted a vast array of foreign officials, including Prime Minister Margaret Thatcher of Great Britain, King Juan Carlos I and Queen Sophia of Spain, President François Mitterrand of France, and in a historic visit, the Soviet leader Mikhail Gorbachev. In the early 1980s the Reagans celebrated the birthdays of former Presidents

Franklin D. Roosevelt and Harry S. Truman and of former First Lady Eleanor Roosevelt at White House luncheons.

George H. W. and Barbara Bush had several official dinners and luncheons, but they often entertained at large receptions. Their traditional style of entertaining was reminiscent of their years of diplomatic service and their lives in Texas and on the Maine coast. In 1989, some four hundred foreign ambassadors and their spouses attended an elegant white-tie reception held in honor of the Washington Diplomatic Corps. Mrs. Bush hosted several receptions in the State Rooms to highlight the work of many nonprofit organizations, and President Bush initiated a presidential lecture series with noted presidential

Trees ablaze with tiny lights offer a glittery backdrop for the barbeque given by President and Mrs. Jimmy Carter on the West Terrace during a visit of the Japanese prime minister in May 1979.

Above: President and
Mrs. Ronald Reagan
with Frank Sinatra
at a White House
performance, 1982.

Right: President
George H. W. Bush
hosts a State
Dinner for Queen
Elizabeth II, 1991.

biographers that was televised from the East Room. In 1992 they presided over the two hundredth anniversary of the laying of the White House cornerstone and submitted letters and mementos for a White House time capsule.

First Lady Hillary Clinton described the White House entertaining style of the Clinton presidency as both "respectful of tradition" and "fun and informal." In November 2000, she and Bill Clinton hosted a historic dinner in the East Room to celebrate the two hundredth anniversary of life in the President's House. With Lady Bird Johnson, Gerald and Betty Ford, Jimmy and Rosalynn Carter, and George H. W. and Barbara Bush in attendance,

President Clinton could announce, "In the entire two hundred years of the White House's history, never before have this many presidents and first ladies gathered in this great room."

A few days earlier, President Clinton had presided over a ceremony marking the arrival of John Adams at the President's House in 1800. "For two centuries now," he stated, "Americans have looked to the White House as a symbol of leadership in times of crisis, of reassurance in times of uncertainty, of continuity in times of change, of celebration in times of joy. . . . We are still in the business of forming that more perfect union of our Founders' dream. I hope and believe John Adams would be pleased."

In celebration of the two hundredth anniversary of the White House, President and Mrs. Bill Clinton hosted a special Anniversary Dinner on November 9, 2000. Their guests included seven former presidents and first ladies. Posing together in the State Dining Room are (left to right): President and Mrs. George H. W. Bush, Lady Bird Johnson, President and Mrs. Clinton, President and Mrs. Gerald R. Ford, and President and Mrs. Jimmy Carter.

Hospitality in the George W. Bush Years

The State Dining Room is set for a dinner celebrating the fortieth anniversary of the National Endowment for the Arts and the National Endowment for the Humanities, 2005.

President George W. and Laura Bush enjoy sharing the White House with guests and the public. Their guest lists have included renowned authors participating in the National Book Festival; writers, historians, and students attending the "Salute to America's Authors" symposia; religious leaders of many faiths; members of Congress and governors; and aspiring ball players and their families coming for tee ball games on the South Lawn. In his second term President and Mrs. Bush have hosted a series of small dinners centered on a particular theme. One featured the works of Shakespeare, with the Aquila Shakespeare Theatre of New York performing scenes from *Much Ado About Nothing* and the White House staff serving food that would have been served in Shakespeare's time.

The Bushes have frequently used the Second Floor of the White House to meet with members of Congress and for special luncheons and dinners. In 2005, they hosted a luncheon for King Harald V and Queen Sonja of Norway in the Yellow Oval Room and a private luncheon for His Royal Highness, Prince Charles of Great Britain, and the Duchess of Cornwall in the Family Dining Room. Especially memorable events on the State Floor have been dinners celebrating President Gerald Ford's ninetieth birthday in 2003 and the sixtieth wedding anniversary of the president's parents in 2005. There were also a Blue Room dinner for the Baseball Hall of Fame and a birthday party in the State Dining Room for Placido Domingo, the

Above: President George W.
Bush and Prime Minister
Junichiro Koizumi of Japan
toast at the start of an
official dinner, 2006.

Left: First Lady Laura Bush
dines with Cherie Blair,
wife of Prime Minister Tony
Blair of Great Britain, in
the Yellow Oval Room on
the Second Floor of the
White House, 2005.

President and Mrs. Bush with guests on the Truman Balcony during the Fourth of July celebration, 2005.

world-renowned tenor and artistic director of the Washington Opera.

Some occasions are much more solemn. President and Mrs. Bush met in the White House with the families of the victims of Flight 93, the plane that crashed in a field in Pennsylvania on September 11, 2001, and with the families of the astronauts who died in the explosion of the space shuttle *Columbia.*

The Truman Balcony, with its breathtaking view of the Washington Monument and the Jefferson Memorial, is the setting each year for the Bushes' Fourth of July celebration. The event is also a way to

celebrate President George W. Bush's birthday on July 6. "We love having close friends come for an Independence Day supper of fried chicken, deviled eggs, and ice cream," Mrs. Bush says, "and then to watch the Fourth of July fireworks display."

To commemorate the three hundredth anniversary of Benjamin Franklin's birthday in 2006, President and Mrs. Bush invited several of his biographers to dinner as well as officials from institutions Franklin had helped found. Foods popular in the eighteenth century were served.

Above: The Bush family poses in the Red Room for a photograph during a celebration of former President and Mrs. George H. W. Bush's sixtieth wedding anniversary.

Left: President and Mrs. Bush, along with Betty Ford, celebrate former President Gerald R. Ford's ninetieth birthday on July 16, 2003.

Holiday Traditions at the White House

President Jimmy Carter poses with his wife, Rosalynn, and daughter, Amy, in front of the Blue Room Christmas tree, 1978.

Not until 1889 did the first Christmas tree appear in the President's House. That year Benjamin and Caroline Harrison, with several grandchildren in residence, placed the tree, lighted with candles, in the oval room on the Second Floor, the family sitting room. Theodore Roosevelt, an ardent conservationist, did not approve of cutting trees, but one year his young children snuck a small tree into the White House to be unveiled on Christmas morning. The first tree to appear on the State Floor was placed in the Blue Room by the Taft children. Most nineteenth- and early twentieth-century presidential families celebrated the holiday with private family festivities on Christmas Day, although an open house on New Year's Day welcomed the public from 1801 to 1932. Like most American homes, the White House in these years was decorated with fresh greens and fruit, but on a simple scale.

Most recently, the White House has been a festive place during the Christmas season, alive with beautiful music and decorations. Mamie Eisenhower had more than twenty-five trees decorated with tinsel and lights placed in the East Room and other areas of the house, including the laundry room. In 1961, Jacqueline Kennedy had the Blue Room tree decorated with ornaments inspired by *The Nutcracker* ballet of Pyotr Tchaikovsky, and that started a tradition. Now each year the first lady selects a special holiday decorating theme, which is documented in detail for television viewers throughout the world. First ladies have borrowed toys from museum

Left: President Lyndon B. Johnson decorates the White House Christmas tree with the help of schoolchildren, 1964.

Below: First Lady Patricia Nixon poses with her White House staff in the Entrance Hall for a holiday photograph, 1973.

Right: First Lady Betty Ford and daughter Susan decorate Christmas cookies in the Solarium on the Third Floor of the White House, 1975.

Below: First Lady Barbara Bush sets the star on top of the National Christmas Tree, 1989; and President and Mrs. Clinton and Chelsea decorate a Christmas tree in the Yellow Oval Room, 1994.

collections, commissioned art school and architectural students, and called on volunteers from the states, territories, and the District of Columbia to make ornaments for the 18-foot high Blue Room tree. Talented and creative needle pointers and crafts people have made thematic ornaments of natural plant materials, paper, fiber, ceramics, metal, and wood.

Laura Bush has chosen a variety of themes. In 2001, with the theme of "Home for the Holidays," models of presidential birthplaces and homes were made for the East Room mantels and tables throughout the public rooms. The next year, "because presidential families have been comforted and entertained by their animal companions," Laura Bush explained, "I chose the theme 'All

Creatures Great and Small.'" Throughout the White House, miniatures and historical photographs of first family pets were the highlights of the holiday display, and the ornaments for the Blue Room tree were representations of birds from each artist's locale. Classic children's stories were featured in 2003 in "A Season of Stories," and in 2004 American Christmas carols were represented in "A Season of Merriment and Melody." The theme for 2005, "All Things Bright and Beautiful," focused on the beauty of the natural world. Members of the White House Executive Residence staff, the National Park Service, and volunteer florists used plants, trees, fruit, and flowers to reflect the country's bounty.

White House pastry chef Roland Mesnier helps guide his 150-pound gingerbread house into the White House, 2001.

Above: First Lady Laura
Bush, next to the Blue
Room Christmas tree,
answers reporters' ques-
tions during a preview of
the 2005 White House
Christmas decorations.

Right: The Bushes' dog
Barney checks to see if
there is a box for him
under the tree.

"The gingerbread White House is always a crowd-pleaser," says Mrs. Bush. This confection, which takes about three weeks to create, is displayed in the State Dining Room. Each year the White House pastry chefs add special touches in keeping with the special theme. The 2006 theme, "Deck the Halls and Welcome All," was captured by a gingerbread South Portico topped with more than 800 hand-piped icing snowflakes.

In 1953, the Eisenhowers sent the first official presidential Christmas cards. Each year, presidential cards, including the most recent, are displayed during the holidays. Harpists, choirs, string ensembles, and other musical groups from across the country add to the joyful holiday spirit for visitors and staff alike. "The whole White House smells like Christmas trees, and the wonderful music puts a smile on every face!" remarks Laura Bush.

Recent presidents have also commemorated the Jewish holiday of Hanukkah, the "Festival of Lights." During the Clinton administration, historic menorahs lent to the White House were lighted and exhibited in the West Wing. Since 2001, they have been on public view in the East Wing, near the entrance to the mansion's Ground Floor. President and Mrs. Bush witness the lighting ceremony and invite all participants to a holiday reception. Following one recent ceremony, as the Marine Band played the music for the hora, participants danced in a circle in the Entrance Hall.

Since the events of September 11, 2001, President George W. Bush has

reached out to the Muslim community by holding a special Iftar dinner to break the daily fast during Ramadan, the holiest month of the Muslim year. Speaking to guests that included foreign ambassadors and American citizens at the first dinner in 2002, the president stated, "America treasures your friendship. America honors your faith." Members of the U.S.-Afghan Women's Council joined Laura Bush for an Iftar dinner in 2005.

Top: First Lady Laura Bush looks on as President George W. Bush helps during the lighting of the menorah in the 2001 Hanukkah ceremony.

Bottom: During the 2005 Iftar dinner, President Bush addresses ambassadors and Muslim leaders in the State Dining Room.

A Marine Band musician plays the Steinway grand piano in the Entrance Hall, 2004.

THE TRADITIONS OF STATE VISITS

President George W. Bush and Philippine President Gloria Macapagal-Arroyo stand for the playing of the national anthems of the United States and the Philippines, during the arrival ceremony on May 19, 2003.

Since World War II, an ever-lengthening procession of foreign leaders has come to 1600 Pennsylvania Avenue to confer on global problems. These dignitaries are often formally entertained at the White House, and an invitation to attend such a function is highly coveted. Certainly a State Dinner to honor a visiting head of government or a reigning monarch is one of the most glamorous of White House affairs, an event that also showcases global power and influence. Today the term "State Dinner" is reserved for events in honor of heads of state, though in the nineteenth century most official dinners, even without a foreign official, were called State Dinners.

Today's State Dinner begins with a morning arrival ceremony that was first

introduced by John F. Kennedy and
remains largely unchanged. In his time,
it also included helicopter service to
transport guests to the Ellipse. Lyndon
Johnson, Richard Nixon, Gerald Ford,
and Jimmy Carter maintained the helicopter arrival, though less frequently, and
the practice has now largely been aban-
doned. Most state guests arrive in
Washington the day before and are driven
through the Southwest Gate toward the
white-columned south entrance of the
White House. There the president and
his wife greet their guests of honor with
a red carpet and often a twenty-one gun
salute. The evening of the State Dinner,
the president and first lady greet their

guests under the North Portico and escort
them to the Yellow Oval Room on the
Second Floor. There they meet with other
top-ranking guests, such as the secretary
of state. Meanwhile, about one hundred
other guests are arriving at the mansion's
east entrance. Passing through the East
Wing, these guests ascend the marble
stairway to the State Floor. On their way
they are presented with cards explaining
seating arrangements. Then they are conducted to the East Room by social aides,
officers chosen from the armed forces. The
president and first lady with their honored
guests descend the Grand Staircase to
the sounds of Ruffles and Flourishes
and then greet the assembled guests in

President George W. Bush
meets with the president
of Liberia, Ellen Johnson-
Sirleaf, in the Oval Office,
2006.

In preparation for a dinner, the East Room piano is tuned (opposite), and the red carpet is placed on the North Portico steps and vacuumed (above).

Right: Tables in the State Dining Room are set with menus, place cards, and floral centerpieces in the shape of elephants in preparation for a dinner with Prime Minister Dr. Manmohan Singh of India.

protocol order. Finally, the president and first lady escort the visitors to the State Dining Room, where the other guests await them.

Decorations and table settings for formal dinners in the White House are classic and elegant. Frequently in use is the set of china acquired during the Reagan administration—red rimmed with a gold band—as well as the Johnson plates, which feature wildflowers, Lady Bird Johnson's favorite motif. In November 2000, President and Mrs. Clinton selected a special set of gold-rimmed ivory china to commemorate the two hundredth anniversary of the White House.

The public does not have to wait long to learn details of the dinner. As an aid to the news media, Lyndon Johnson had an electronic system installed so that reporters assembled in another room could hear the traditional toasts exchanged by the two heads of state. More recently, some foreign leaders have arranged for coverage of the dinners for later television broadcast in their home countries. Newscasts and next-day newspapers often carry pictures and stories on the guests, menu, and entertainment. To obtain such information and to add firsthand descriptions to their coverage, a few White House reporters have long been permitted to attend the after-dinner entertainment and to chat with the guests.

Behind the glitter and ceremony of such state affairs is elaborate planning that tailors each aspect of the event to the national cultures and individual tastes of the guests of honor. These formal dinners involve the creation of guest lists, menus, flowers, table settings, and entertainment for the evening. To assure the success of the meal, the Reagans even tried out the complete dinner, down to the last detail, a week or ten days before the event.

When, on September 5, 2001, Mexican President Vicente Fox and his wife Marta Sahagún Fox made the first state visit to the White House during the presidency of George W. Bush, the U.S. Marine Band played the Mexican national anthem, followed by the national anthem of the United States at the morning arrival ceremony. The U.S. Army Old Guard Fife and Drum Corps marched in review on the broad expanse of the South Lawn before President Bush pronounced an official welcome and President Fox responded with a speech that reflected the ties between Mexico and the United States. The menu for the State Dinner was planned to combine American specialties with Mexican flavors. President Fox and his guests enjoyed Maryland crab and chorizo pozole followed by pepita-crusted bison. For dessert, the White House pastry chef created a masterpiece mango and coconut ice cream dome with peaches.

First Lady Laura Bush works closely with the White House social secretary and the Executive Residence staff to coordinate every detail for such special occasions, and Executive Chef Cristeta Comerford prepares special menus. The State Department provides the White House

chefs with the guests' dietary preferences and restrictions. For the dinner for Indian Prime Minister Manmohan Singh, guests enjoyed chilled asparagus soup and halibut and basmati rice with pistachio nuts and currants. The pastry chef prepared mango, chocolate-cardamom and cashew ice creams with chocolate lotus blossoms for dessert.

President and Mrs. Bush have also hosted state visits at the White House for the presidents of Poland, the Philippines, and Kenya, and official dinners for the retiring president of the Czech Republic, Václav Havel, the prime minister of India,

and the Australian prime minister, John Howard. With the increased interest of foreign dignitaries in visiting the White House, especially after the events of September 11, 2001, President Bush has preferred to host regular working lunches and dinners for heads of state and government in the Family Dining Room and the Bushes' private residence, holding more than sixty such events in his first term. These visits often begin in the Oval Office, followed by additional meetings in the Cabinet Room with members of both the United States and foreign delegations.

President and Mrs. George W. Bush, welcome the Prince of Wales and Duchess of Cornwall to the White House, 2005.

SHOWCASE PERFORMANCES

American musicians have performed at the White House for more than two hundred years, and the showcase performances have often reflected the musical tastes of first families or their guests. The Marine Band has been a presence at the President's House since it first played for John and Abigail Adams's New Year's Day reception in 1801, and many other military groups such as the Air Force Strolling Strings and the Army and Navy Choruses have performed.

Jefferson considered music "the favorite passion of my soul" and often played the violin, as did another Virginian, John Tyler. Dolley Madison purchased the first piano for the house, and James Monroe ordered one from Paris in 1817. Louisa Adams played the harp; Caroline Harrison and Florence Harding were professional musicians. Lincoln loved opera, Franklin D. Roosevelt enjoyed folk music, Truman and Nixon played the piano, and Clinton played the saxophone.

Music ranging from classical, folk, and country to gospel, opera, and jazz has all been heard in the East Room or on the South Lawn. Often, performers visiting Washington are invited to perform for the president, his family and guests. Beginning in the 1840s, the Hutchison family singers went on to sing for seven presidents. In 1882, the Fisk Jubilee Singers sang for Chester Arthur. Edith Roosevelt initiated a series of classical music recitals; the cellist Pablo Casals performed one evening in 1904 and returned

Left: Former President Harry S. Truman performs in the East Room of the White House during the Kennedy administration, 1961.

Above: The United States Army Old Guard Fife and Drum Corps perform during a re-enactment of the arrival of President John Adams at the White House on the two hundredth anniversary of the event in November 2000.

more than fifty years later to play for
President and Mrs. Kennedy and their
guests. When Franklin D. Roosevelt and
Eleanor Roosevelt entertained the king
and queen of England in 1939, they
included a concert of American music
that highlighted folk and concert musicians. Among the performers were Kate
Smith, the North Carolina Spiritual
Singers, and Marian Anderson. Nixon
hosted a special dinner for Duke
Ellington's seventieth birthday in 1969
and, at the after dinner concert, sat down
at the White House Steinway to play
"Happy Birthday" to him.

John and Jacqueline Kennedy
brought some of the finest artists to the
White House to "demonstrate that the
White House could be an influence in
encouraging public acceptance of the

arts," according to a 1962 newspaper
report. Their programs often reflected
the first lady's cultured tastes. The
Kennedys also initiated a series of
"Concerts for Young People by Young
People." At one of them opera singer
Grace Brumby, just 25 years old, made
her American debut in 1961, to rave
reviews.

Jimmy and Rosalynn Carter demonstrated their love of classical music by
establishing a series of concerts titled "In
Performance at the White House" that
has been broadcast over public television
from the East Room. Rosalynn Carter
explained that the idea for this program
"came about because Jimmy and I knew
there were so many people who had never
been to the White House. . . . We wanted
all of America to enjoy the White House

Above: Cellist Yo-Yo Ma and pianist Kathryn Scott provide after-dinner entertainment for the dinner in honor of Charles, Prince of Wales and Camilla, Duchess of Cornwall, 2005.

Right: First Lady Laura Bush stands with members of the cast from the Tony Award-winning musical *Jersey Boys,* during a Senate spouses luncheon, 2006.

as we did." The distinguished pianist Vladimir Horowitz opened the series, followed by Mstislav Rostropovich, Leontyne Price, Mikhail Baryshnikov, and Andrés Segovia.

The first public television concert hosted by George W. and Laura Bush was a salute to the Marine Band known as "the President's Own." Larry Gatlin and Gerald McRaney were the masters of ceremonies, and performers included Nell Carter and Toby Keith as well as the Marine Band itself. President and Mrs. Bush have continued the "In Performance at the White House" series and have invited some of America's greatest musical talents to perform for honored guests at State Dinners. Dawn Upshaw sang during the dinner for

Mexico; jazz singer Vanessa Rubin entertained during the dinner for Poland; the Alvin Ailey American Dance Theater performed for Kenya; and the Preservation Hall Jazz Band performed for India. During the annual dinner for the nation's governors, Bernadette Peters, Lee Ann Womack, Lyle Lovett, Natalie Cole, Mark McVey, and Marvin Hamlisch have delighted all those in attendance. The legendary B. B. King brought the house down when he entertained a group from the Special Olympics. In 2005, Cherish the Ladies performed at a Saint Patrick's Day dinner, and the sounds of Los Mariachis del Sol were heard at a Cinco de Mayo dinner. Musical performances at the White House continue to reflect the sounds of America.

B. B. King performs in the East Room in a celebration of Black History Month focusing on music of the Gulf Coast, 2006.

The First Family at Home

3

Despite all the comforts and privileges that come to a president and his family, living in a house that is also a national monument has its challenges. When Calvin Coolidge arrived at the White House in 1923, he tried to continue his after-dinner habit of sitting on his front porch, watching people go by. But so many stopped to stare at him that he gave up this pleasant relaxation. To have a personal life in such a place is a struggle. Indeed, the attention commanded by the presidency intensifies the normal joys and sorrows of everyday family experience, the high moments of birth and the despair of death that are part of life here as in any other home.

As husband and father, nearly every president has known the frustration, especially in periods of national stress, of trying to find enough time to be with his family. When James Garfield's son Harry was 17 and fell in love with the daughter of one of his father's best friends, a month passed before young Garfield was able to get the president alone to talk about it. Eleanor Roosevelt wrote that at times the Roosevelt boys had to make appointments to see their father. "I doubt if the public realizes," she observed, "the price that the whole family pays in curtailment of opportunity to live a close family life."

President and Mrs. Calvin Coolidge with sons Calvin and John on the South Portico of the White House, 1924.

First Ladies on a National Stage

First Lady Edith Wilson assists her husband President Woodrow Wilson at his desk in June 1920.

Accentuated challenges, too, face each first lady in her highly visible role as the president's wife and the person responsible for overseeing the management of a national historic house. The public is keenly interested in, and often feels free to voice opinions on the projects she chooses to support and the way she runs the house, selects her clothes, or chooses to style her hair. Lou Hoover told of receiving a letter from an indignant tourist who complained about a mended curtain she had seen in one of the rooms. Eleanor Roosevelt remarked that she sometimes felt she was no longer clothing herself "but dressing a public monument."

The clothes and styles of a president's wife may sway fashions everywhere. Jacqueline Kennedy's style was copied around the world. When designers drastically lengthened skirts in 1970, reporters asked Pat Nixon just how far from the floor she would wear her hems. Betty Ford, who made her living as a model when she was a young woman studying dance, stayed in step with—and sometimes ahead of—current vogues. Some of Rosalynn Carter's clothes came from top American designers, but she also brought her own sewing machine with her to the White House. Nancy Reagan, who favored classic daytime suits and elegant evening gowns, endured some criticism for her large wardrobe of designer clothes.

In John Adams's time, critics felt that witty, politically sophisticated Abigail had too much influence on the president. To one of them she was "Her Majesty" and

"Mrs. President." After that, and throughout the nineteenth century, most wives avoided a political role, limiting themselves to charity and to mild support of such broad issues as temperance and women's suffrage. Dolley Madison helped found and direct a capital orphanage, to which she was said to have contributed "$20 and a cow." Sarah Polk worked as the president's private secretary, clipping and summarizing war news and political reports for him. In the early twentieth century Edith Wilson protected her ill husband by screening his visitors and official papers so persistently that critics called her "Mrs. President," too. Florence Harding, who had worked with her husband at his Ohio newspaper, advised him during his 1920 election campaign. In the White House, she made herself accessible to the press and was the first first lady to give radio interviews. A former teacher of the deaf, Grace Coolidge had a warm personality and interest in people that complemented her taciturn husband in the political milieu of Washington. Lou Hoover, well educated, well traveled, and with broad interests, was long active in the Girl Scouts and served as its president while her husband was secretary of commerce.

The first wife of a president to participate actively in national affairs was Eleanor Roosevelt. She offered the first press conferences for newswomen, produced prime news during these sessions, and wrote a newspaper column for years. She traveled so much on lecture tours, visits to overseas troops, and as the "eyes and ears" of FDR that her White House code name was "Rover."

Since then, many of America's first ladies have stepped up to the podium to help shape the presidency and the nation. They have their own staff support to assist with projects, handle press inquiries and correspondence, and plan social events, unlike many nineteenth-century first ladies, who had to call on daughters and friends to address invitations to White House social events.

First Lady Eleanor Roosevelt with her secretary, Malvina Thompson (left), and social secretary, Edith Helm, in a study on the Second Floor of the White House, 1941.

Above: Surrounded by schoolchildren, First Lady Patricia Nixon views a presentation of the "Summer in the Parks" program, 1970.

Opposite: First Lady Lady Bird Johnson meets in the Treaty Room with her Committee for a More Beautiful Capital, 1966.

Jacqueline Kennedy hired the first press secretary on the first lady's staff. With the increasing public interest in her efforts to make the White House a place filled with the echoes of past residents and the finest American works of art and furnishings, she also appointed the first curator to oversee the museum functions of the President's House.

Lady Bird Johnson turned out to be another "Woman Doer," to use the title she created to honor outstanding women, including those active in her own programs to beautify the landscape and to give needy children a preschool boost to education through Head Start. Patricia Nixon emphasized volunteer work and became a goodwill ambassador to Latin America in 1970. After an earthquake

shook a vast area of Peru, she flew into the devastated region in a cargo plane carrying emergency supplies.

Betty Ford, with her personal warmth and interest in people, made friends for her husband and her country as she traveled with him at home and abroad. She gave strong support to women's issues and the performing arts. Rosalynn Carter embarked on many far-reaching programs, including a national drive to improve the care of the mentally ill. Nancy Reagan worked to fight drug abuse among children. Barbara Bush devoted much time to promoting literacy. Hillary Rodham Clinton advocated human rights, health care, historic preservation, and economic empowerment for women on her goodwill trips abroad. In 2000 she was

First Lady Betty Ford greets a blind March of Dimes poster child during a White House event, 1974.

First Lady Barbara Bush gives a lifesaving award to a school safety patrol member, 1991.

First Lady Rosalynn
Carter reports to the
President's Commission
on Mental Health, 1978.

First Lady Nancy Reagan
presides over a confer-
ence on drug abuse in
the East Room, April
1985.

First Lady Hillary Rodham Clinton speaks on health care reform on the South Lawn of the White House, September 1993.

elected to the U.S. Senate by the State of New York.

Laura Bush likes to quote Lady Bird Johnson, one of the first ladies she most admires, who said, "The Constitution of the United States does not mention the first lady. One man elects her only. The statute books assign her no duties; and yet, when she gets the job, a podium is there if she cares to use it." As a former public school teacher and librarian with a passion for reading, education, and promoting opportunities for women around the world, Mrs. Bush visits many schools, reading to children and talking to them about the importance of a good education. One of her top priorities is making sure that parents and caregivers know the most

effective ways to prepare young children to be ready to learn to read when they enter school. Two White House symposia reflected Mrs. Bush's lifelong interest in childhood development issues. The White House Summit on Early Childhood Cognitive Development emphasized preparing young children for school and lifetime learning. At the White House Conference on Helping America's Youth, speakers discussed the challenges children and teenagers face and ways communities can address them. This event was a part of an initiative announced by President George W. Bush in 2005, which he asked Mrs. Bush to lead.

To share the joy of books and reading with all ages, Laura Bush and the Library of

Congress hosted the first National Book Festival in Washington, D.C., in September 2001. Bringing together major American authors who gather at the White House before the readings and book-signings on the National Mall, the National Book Festival draws tens of thousands of book lovers every September. Mrs. Bush has also hosted authors and scholars at White House events honoring Mark Twain, William Shakespeare, women writers of the American West, and the Harlem Renaissance.

In February 2003, the United Nations launched the International Decade of Literacy and named Laura Bush its Honorary Ambassador. In September 2006, during the opening of the sixty first U.N. General Assembly, Mrs. Bush hosted a White House Conference on Global Literacy in New York. The conference gathered first ladies, education ministers, and literacy experts from across the globe to highlight the international benefits of reading, and issued a call to governments everywhere to improve literacy rates in their countries.

Mrs. Bush also pays close attention to events in Afghanistan. In 2001, she became the only first lady ever to record a full radio address to the nation, speaking about the plight of women and children under the oppressive Taliban regime. She later visited Afghanistan to underscore the nation's progress and welcomes Afghan teachers to the White House each year.

First Lady Laura Bush receives a T-shirt from Aunt Manyongo "Kunene" Mosima Tantoh, a representative of South Africa's Mothers-to-Mothers Program, which helps HIV-positive pregnant women avoid transmitting the disease to their unborn children, March 2006.

CHILDREN AT THE WHITE HOUSE

One of the most endearing aspects of life in the Executive Mansion can be glimpsed from the hundreds of stories that have come down through the years about the many children who have lived, and sometimes grown up, in the White House, where something new and exciting is always happening.

The very young ones were usually grandchildren, since few men have reached the top rung of the political ladder in their early years. And the first of all these children whose shouts and laughter echoed through the mansion's broad corridors was the four-year-old granddaughter of John and Abigail Adams. Little Susanna arrived in November 1800 in the carriage bringing her grandmother, who was belatedly joining President Adams in the unfinished building. The little girl distressed her grandparents soon afterward by developing whooping cough, but she recovered and lived to tell her own small granddaughter Susanna of her adventures in the White House.

Thomas Jefferson's eight years in the presidency were cheered and brightened by the visits of his married daughters, Martha Randolph and Maria Eppes. On one of these visits, in the winter of 1805, Mrs. Randolph gave birth to her eighth child—named James Madison Randolph. It is probable that the first child born here was to Ursula Hughes, a slave, in 1802. Five children of African American servants were born in the President's House during Jefferson's time. In her chronicles of early Washington life, Margaret Bayard Smith recalled

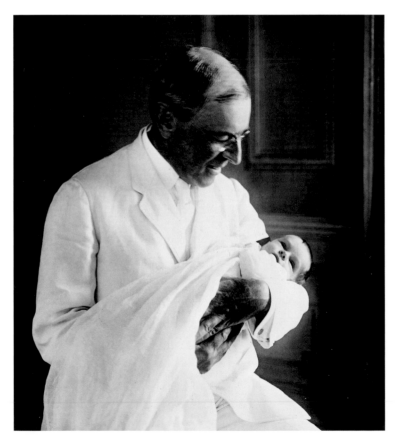

Opposite: First Lady Frances Cleveland poses with baby Marion at the White House, 1896.

Above: President Woodrow Wilson with his first grandchild, Ellen Wilson McAdoo, in his arms, 1915.

Jefferson's remark when she mentioned the amusement that children afforded adults. "Yes," he said, "it is only with them that a grave man can play the fool."

Though Andrew and Rachel Jackson never had children of their own, the widowed president surrounded himself with Rachel's visiting nieces and nephews and their offspring. Three of the six or more youngsters usually on hand were born in the White House. They were children of Rachel's nephew Andrew Jackson Donelson, who stayed with the president as his private secretary, and his wife, Emily, who served as Jackson's official hostess.

"Uncle Andrew," as the children called the president, often attended personally to the needs and wants of his adopted family; he rolled their baby carriages through the halls, comforted them in teething, and frequently joined in their games. Golden-haired Mary Emily Donelson wrote long afterward about a happy Christmas season she spent with the president and of a party that Jackson gave for the youngsters, their playmates, and other Washington children. Though the world knew him as a man of "iron will and fierce, ungovernable temper," she said, "he was the gentlest, tenderest, most patient of men at his own fireside."

It may surprise many who recall pictures of Abraham Lincoln's lined and aging face that he and his wife, 52 and 43 respectively, were among the youngest presidential couples, and that they were the first to bring to the White House a child of their own who was under 10.

Thomas, or "Tad," was 7, William 10, and their brother Robert, who would be off at college most of the time, 17, when Lincoln and his family arrived in Washington from Illinois, to be at the center of the nation's most tragic era.

Abraham and Mary Lincoln were loving and indulgent parents who often said, "Let the children have a good time." This the children did, and the president's friends and colleagues quite probably felt he was too permissive at times, as when he failed to punish Tad for bombarding the door with his toy cannon during a cabinet meeting or when the boy stopped his father's callers to sell refreshments and wheedle money for war charities at stands he set up at the mansion. But the president found Tad's pranks a welcome relief from sorrow and responsibility, and he took pride in Tad's generous nature, as well as in the talent that gentle, cheerful Willie revealed in the verses and short speeches he composed.

Lincoln thoroughly enjoyed, too, the physical activity of a good wrestling match with his boys, and he encouraged them in the fun of collecting and raising pets of various kinds, including dogs, ponies, and goats. Lincoln bought Tad a pair of goats at $5 each. He got his money's worth in amusement when the youngster hitched the animals to a kitchen chair and drove his unlikely rig through the East Room, to the consternation of a group of visiting ladies from Boston. When one of the goats disappeared, Lincoln wrote a whimsical letter saying "poor Nanny" had last been

Young Tad Lincoln, seen photographed in 1864 in a lieutenant's uniform, was given a courtesy commission by Secretary of War Edwin M. Stanton.

seen "chewing her little cud, on the middle of Tad's bed."

Ulysses and Julia Grant, the next couple to arrive at the Executive Mansion with young children of their own, were fortunate in leading one of the happiest and most normal of family lives in the history of the White House. Their affectionate and outgoing children—three sons and a daughter named Nellie—ranged in age from 11 to 18. The middle son, Ulysses Simpson Jr., was called "Buck" because he was born in the Buckeye State of Ohio. Both he and his older brother, Frederick, worked for the president as confidential secretaries during Grant's second term.

One of the liveliest and warmest accounts of the Grants comes from the fun-loving youngest son, Jesse. In his book of reminiscences, *In the Days of My Father, General Grant,* he told of his joy in the gift of a small but powerful telescope, which he used to study the heavens. He recalled the gatherings of neighborhood friends who "flocked to the White House . . . the largest and best playground available." The "lot was our playground, in good weather," he wrote, "the big, airy basement . . . was reserved for rain or storm."

Jesse also became an ardent stamp collector. In his impatience to receive an order that he had paid for with $5 out of his savings, he appealed to his father, suggesting that the secretary of state write to the dealer, or the secretary of war could write, or Kelly, a policeman on White House duty. The matter was solemnly debated at a cabinet meeting, with Jesse pleading his case. It was finally decided to have Kelly write the following: "I am a Capitol Policeman. I can arrest anybody, anywhere, at any time, for anything. I want you to send those stamps to Jesse Grant right at once." The stamps came. Wrote Jesse in memory of his family: "The love of my parents for each other and their devotion to us children made no impression on me then. I had never known anything different. Appreciation and understanding come to me now, filling me with content."

Following Grant, both Rutherford B. Hayes and James A. Garfield brought warmhearted, close-knit families to the Executive Mansion. Each included four boys and a girl. Moreover, the two families were old friends, linked by common Ohio origins and congressional service in Washington. Fanny Hayes and Mollie Garfield, both 14, sat together at Garfield's inauguration, behind the mother of the president-elect—the first mother to see her son take the oath of office. Mollie continued her friendship with Fanny after the family, including Grandmother Garfield, moved into the mansion. When Mollie gave a luncheon for 10 young girls, she remembered her obligations as a hostess in the White House and seated Fanny, as the daughter of a past president, on her right.

Garfield's two older sons, Harry and James, stayed at the White House with their family, studying there under a private tutor instead of completing the remaining months of their prep-school terms. Thus

they, too, happened to be with the rest of the family, along with Mollie and the two younger boys, Irvin and Abram, during most of the last six months of their father's life. He was shot in 1881.

The most photographed presidential grandchild of the nineteenth century must have been "Baby McKee," who lived in the White House with grandfather Benjamin Harrison and his four-generation family during the early 1890s. Among the numerous family members, which included parents, grandparents, aunt, uncle, cousins, and great-grandfather, mischievous little Benjamin gained a reputation with the press as the president's favorite who could do no wrong.

Professional and amateur photographers were just then discovering George Eastman's new, easy-to-operate Kodak box camera—one of the first to use roll film—and they haunted the grounds, hoping to get pictures of little Benjamin. Published photographs soon showed the active and appealing youngster as he played with his dog, led the Marine Band, or drove his own goat cart about the grounds.

The goat, called His Whiskers by the coachman, once ran away with Baby McKee, giving reporters one of their best stories about him. As His Whiskers darted off with the boy down the White House driveway onto Pennsylvania Avenue, the portly president himself, dressed in top hat and frock coat, followed in hot pursuit.

With such a start in the 1890s, illustrated news coverage of the younger

members of the chief executive's family has never slackened.

In 1893 Esther Cleveland, the second daughter of Grover and Frances Cleveland, was born in the mansion, the only president's child to have that distinction. Esther's sister Ruth, who had arrived during the interlude between Cleveland's two terms, was almost two years old at the time of Esther's birth. Before the president's second term ended, another little girl, Marion, was born at the Cleveland's summer home in Massachusetts.

"The Cleveland children were . . . much beloved by everyone around the place," wrote durable Chief Usher Ike Hoover, who would serve in ten administrations. "We often wished that more of them had been born in the White House." The public seemed to feel the same way about the three pretty little girls. Gifts and advice on how to rear them poured into the White House from all over the country.

One Washington boy organized what he called an honor guard for Ruth. Marching his young company up to the door, he asked for, and received, an interview with the president. Cleveland regretted he was too busy to review the troops, but he delegated the role to Mrs. Cleveland, who

Baby McKee holds the reins of His Whiskers, a goat presented to him by his grandfather, President Benjamin Harrison, c. 1892.

Four generations of President Benjamin Harrison's family posed at the White House for this photograph in 1889: his wife Caroline Harrison, daughter Mary McKee, grandchildren Benjamin Harrison McKee (Baby McKee) and Mary L. McKee, along with Reverend Dr. Scott (Mrs. Harrison's father).

complied with pleasure. Another, less pleasant, incident occurred when a group of curious visitors gathered around Ruth and her nurse during an outing on the grounds. One of the women picked up the child and passed her around to the accompaniment of pats and kisses. The episode so alarmed Mrs. Cleveland that from then on the gates to the South Lawn were closed to the public—an exclusion that resulted in cruel and baseless rumors that the child was deformed.

Four and a half years after the departure of the demure little Cleveland girls, the uninhibited children of Theodore Roosevelt came on with the force of a hurricane. "A nervous person had no business around the White House in those days," observed Ike Hoover in describing their behavior. "Places that had not seen a human being for years were now made alive with the howls and laughter of these new-comers. . . . Nothing was too sacred for their amusement and no place too good for a playroom."

Among other pranks, the five younger children—aged 3 to 14 when the Roosevelts arrived—slid down the stairways on trays stolen from the pantry, stalked the halls on stilts, and bicycled and skated on newly polished floors. Speeding in his toy wagon, Quentin, the youngest, rammed the full-length portrait of Lucy Webb Hayes, leaving a hole.

The boys' lovely, self-willed half sister, Alice, then 17, contributed to the uproar in her own way. She refused to go away to boarding school, but she later

made trips around the country, as well as to Cuba, Puerto Rico, and Asia. From shipboard in the Pacific came the story that "Princess Alice" had jumped, fully dressed, into the ship's pool.

"I can do one of two things," the president once said. "I can be President of the United States, or I can control Alice."

The Roosevelt children also kept a small zoo of pets. Underfoot, inside and out, were a badger, a bear, raccoons, rabbits, turtles, parrots, pigs, cats, dogs, rats, guinea pigs, snakes, and a calico pony named Algonquin. When Archie had the measles, his brothers entertained him by leading the pony into his Second Floor bedroom, after riding up in the president's elevator.

When Quentin grew old enough, he was sent to a nearby public school, and he often brought his pals home to add to the commotion. One of these friends, Earle Looker, many years later wrote a book called *The White House Gang.* In it he described the hilarious adventures of the boys and the quick and just punishment meted out by the president after such antics as the spattering of Andrew Jackson's portrait with spitballs.

TR, as the gang called him—not disrespectfully but with a mixture of affection and awe—had an amazing knowledge of the interests and needs of active children. When official business was slow, he sometimes joined the youngsters for games in the White House attic. On one such occasion, as the president was about to catch up with a boy he was

Above: The six children of President and Mrs. Theodore Roosevelt filled the White House with their boisterous activity and many pets. Posing with the White House police during roll call, Archie salutes while Quentin stands at ease, 1902.

Left: Theodore Roosevelt Jr. holds a pet macaw, 1902.

Opposite: The president poses with his sons Archie and Quentin, 1904.

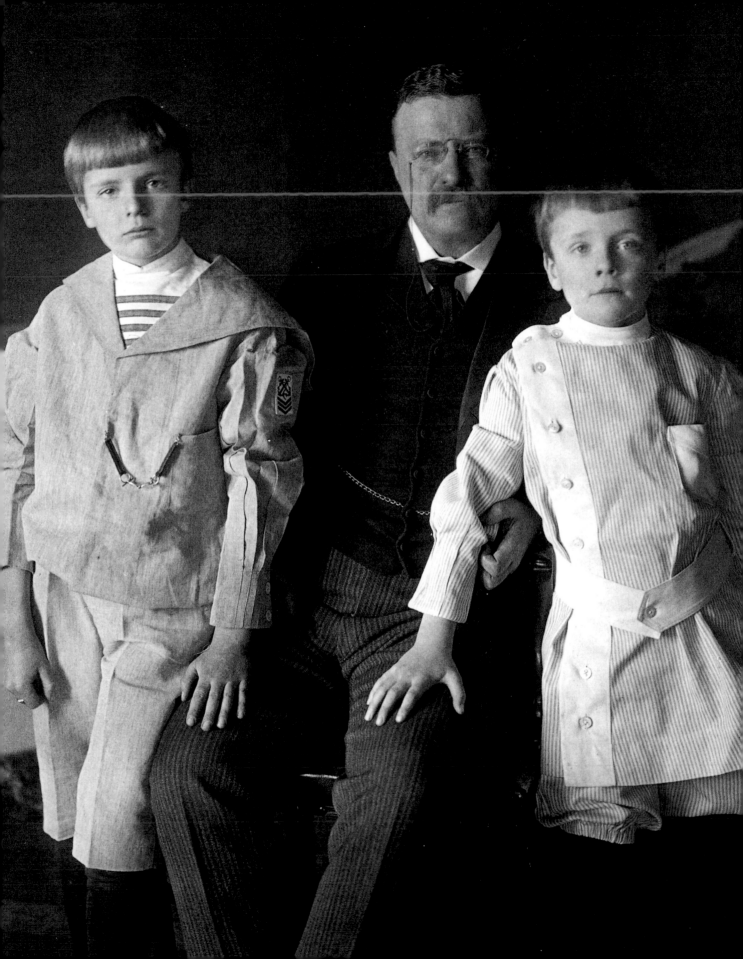

President William Howard Taft and his children, Charlie and Helen, on horseback, c. 1909.

chasing, young Earle turned out the light. A crash followed, and when Earle found the switch again, he saw Roosevelt holding his head and leaning against a post, from which a nail protruded shockingly close to the height of his eyes. "I'm quite all right," he told the contrite boys, "but never, n-e-v-e-r, never again, turn off a light when anybody is near a post!"

Mrs. Roosevelt managed to preside with grace and calm over her large, boisterous group of children, and TR once summed up his feelings in a letter to their son Kermit: "I don't think that any family has ever enjoyed the White House more than we have."

When the Tafts moved into the White House in 1909, their daughter, Helen,

18 at the time, often assisted her mother as hostess, while her younger brother, Charles, 12, was as active as the Roosevelt children. Their older brother, Robert, was often away at school.

Next came the three daughters of Woodrow and Ellen Wilson—Margaret, Jessie, and Eleanor. Though Wilson often appeared to outsiders as the perfect example of the austere, erudite professor, in his close-knit and affectionate family circle he was a jaunty, fun-loving man who was fond of group singing, impersonations, and limericks. The Wilson daughters supported their ill mother, who died in the White House in 1914. The two Coolidge sons, John and Calvin Jr., away at school most of the year, had a brief time together

Above: First Lady Ellen Wilson, with daughters Jessie, Margaret, and Nell, on the South Portico, 1913.

Left: President Franklin Roosevelt's grandchildren, Sistie (Eleanor Dall Seagraves) and Buzzie (Curtis) Dall, play on the South Lawn, 1933.

in the White House before Calvin Jr., 16, died of blood poisoning in 1924.

Stories and pictures of Franklin Roosevelt's grandchildren Anna Eleanor and Curtis Dall made their nicknames, "Sistie" and "Buzzie," household words throughout the country during their stay in the White House. In January 1945, all thirteen of his grandchildren attended his historic fourth inauguration—the largest group of grandchildren ever assembled at the Executive Mansion.

In their time, Dwight D. and Mamie Eisenhower delighted in the visits of their four grandchildren—David, Barbara Anne, Susan, and Mary Jean. Though none of these children of John and Barbara Eisenhower actually lived in the White House, the youngest, Mary Jean, was christened in the Blue Room, and all found plenty of toys and playground equipment on hand for their amusement. The children called their grandmother "Mimi," and a revealing story shows how they regarded Grandfather Eisenhower. Someone had asked small David his name. "Dwight David Eisenhower," he replied. "Then who's that?" probed the questioner, pointing to the president. "That's Ike," said the boy.

Ten administrations would follow that of Grover Cleveland before the cry of a president's infant was again heard inside the Executive Mansion. Then, early in 1961, came John and Jacqueline Kennedy with their two-month-old baby, John Jr., and his engaging sister, Caroline, three years old. Soon newspaper and magazine

editors were publishing stories and pictures of the youngsters' Third Floor playroom, where the Eisenhower grandchildren had romped not long before. There were also stories about the new tree house, swings, and other playground equipment behind South Lawn shrubbery, and about Caroline's pet canary Robin, her pony Macaroni, and her dog Pushinka, the gift of Soviet Premier Nikita Khrushchev.

Fond anecdotes told how "John-John" had refused to greet the Grand Duchess of Luxembourg because he had not been given his usual cookie and ginger ale; how Caroline had presented India's Prime Minister Jawaharlal Nehru with a rose for his buttonhole; and what she said when reporters asked what her father was doing. "Oh, he's upstairs with

his shoes and socks off," she said, "not doing anything." As a child of the Space Age, Caroline Kennedy made news again when she asked John Glenn not about his pioneering flight around the Earth but about another orbital test with chimpanzees. "Where's the monkey?" she asked the astronaut.

By restricting photographs and limiting access to her children, Mrs. Kennedy sought to protect them from the effects of so much concentrated attention. She established a kindergarten at home, as had Mrs. Cleveland, so that Caroline and little John could play with children of their own age, away from the public eye.

The two teenage daughters of President and Mrs. Lyndon B. Johnson, Luci, a high school student, and Lynda, a college student, brought a different liveliness to the Executive Mansion. Of dating age, they had to adjust to life in the public eye. Both married while in the White House. Of the same generation, Julie and Tricia Nixon, too, learned to live both private and public lives. Julie and her husband, David Eisenhower, the grandson of Ike, lived at the White House from time to time; she was an articulate defender of her father during the Watergate crisis. Tricia lived with her parents in the White House until her marriage in 1971.

The Gerald Fords had a teenage daughter, Susan, when they took up residence in 1974. In her last year of high school, she held her senior prom in the East Room. The three older sons— Michael, Jack, and Steven—with careers

of their own, often spent time in the mansion.

Amy Carter, 10 years old when her father assumed office, captured the attention of the nation. The youngest of the Carter offspring, Amy was by far the best known. Her tree house in the gnarled old cedar on the South Lawn, her delight in reading, her violin lessons, pets, and school friends became part of the continuing White House chronicles that began with Susanna, granddaughter of John and Abigail Adams. Two of her older brothers,

Above: First Lady Rosalynn Carter listens while daughter Amy practices the violin, 1979.

Right: President George H. W. Bush visits with his granddaughter Marshall in the Oval Office, 1991.

Chip and Jeff, lived with their families in Third Floor suites; the oldest son, Jack, and his family came for special occasions.

Ronald Reagan's oldest daughter, Maureen, a strong supporter of her father, stayed at the White House often while lending support to her father's agenda. Son Michael and his children, the president's grandchildren, came for special holidays and events, as did Patricia and Ron Jr.

In the late 1980s, George and Barbara Bush's extended family of four sons (including a future president) and a daughter, with their children, frequently spent time at the White House. They were active users of the White House swimming pool, tennis courts, and horseshoe pit.

A young teenager, Chelsea Clinton, 13, grew into a young woman during the eight years of her father's presidency. Her friends were often there to join her in the swimming pool or in the White House movie theater. She studied ballet, attended high school, and led a normal life out of the spotlight.

George W. and Laura Bush's twin daughters — Barbara and Jenna — entered their first year of college in 2000, months before their family moved into the White House. After their graduations in 2004, they joined their father at campaign events and accompanied their mother on foreign trips.

President George W. Bush with wife Laura and daughters Jenna and Barbara in the West Sitting Hall, 2004.

WHITE HOUSE PETS

Right: First Lady Grace Coolidge holds a pet raccoon named Rebecca, c. 1925.

Below: President Richard M. Nixon introduces his new dog Timahoe to the press on January 28, 1969. The Irish Setter was named after a town in County Kildare, Ireland, where Nixon's ancestors lived.

Below: Amy Carter with her dog, Grits, who was given to her by her teacher. In addition to Grits, the Carters had a cat, Misty Malarky Ying Yang.

Above: President Lyndon Johnson and Yuki sing in the Oval Office. Yuki was found at a Texas gas station by Johnson's daughter Luci.

Left: President Ronald Reagan and Prime Minister Margaret Thatcher try to keep up with Lucky, President Reagan's Bouvier des Flandres sheepdog, 1985.

Bottom left: Liberty joins President Gerald Ford in the Oval Office as he works on the budget in November 1974.

Bottom right: Chelsea Clinton and cat Socks visit the president in the Oval Office before a last-minute shopping trip on Christmas Eve, 1994.

WHITE HOUSE WEDDINGS

In 1812 Dolley Madison arranged the first nuptials held at the White House— the wedding of her widowed sister, Lucy Payne Washington, to "the estimable and amiable" Supreme Court Justice Thomas Todd. According to one observer, charming Dolley innocently held the spotlight, "looking every inch the queen."

When James and Elizabeth Monroe announced plans in 1820 for the first White House wedding for a presidential daughter, Maria Monroe, not yet 17, to her cousin and father's secretary, Samuel Laurence Gouverneur, a tempest brewed. The ceremony would be private, the family decreed. Foreign diplomats were pointedly advised "to take no notice" of the event. Afterward, Mrs. William Winston Seaton, wife of a prominent Washington newspaper editor, commented, "The New York style was adopted. . . . Only the attendants, the relations, and a few old friends of the bride and groom witnessed the ceremony."

The John Quincy Adams family also held a historic wedding. On February 25, 1828, young John Adams, grandson of one president and son of another, married his cousin Mary Catherine Hellen, who had lived with the family in the White House. The event marks the only time that a president's son has been wed in the mansion. The ceremony was held in the First Floor oval room—now the Blue Room—which was then decorated in crimson and gold. It was not an altogether happy occasion for the Adams

Opposite: President Theodore Roosevelt with his daughter Alice and her husband Nicholas Longworth, on the day of their East Room wedding, February 17, 1906.

Above: A medallion depicting President James Monroe's daughter, Maria Hester Monroe. She was married at the White House in 1820.

Invited guests view the wedding presents given to President Ulysses S. Grant's daughter Nellie, 1874.

family. The president had disapproved of the match, probably because Mary Catherine had flirted earlier with John's two brothers. But the reception provided a bright note to an otherwise gloomy election year. Even the reserved and formal president danced the Virginia reel.

Letitia Tyler, wife of John Tyler, appeared in company only once in the White House, at the wedding of her daughter, Elizabeth, to William Waller of Virginia in 1842. Wearing a simple gown and a soft lace cap that framed her dark eyes, she sat quietly during the festivities. "Lizzie has had quite a grand wedding," Mrs. Robert Tyler wrote of the event, which all Washington society attended. Dolley Madison, now 73 and popular as ever, was there, as well as the eloquent Daniel Webster, Tyler's secretary of state and a great friend of the family. In his deep, resonant voice, Webster quoted Sir Walter Scott when someone remarked that the president's pretty daughter was giving up capital "belleship" to live in quiet Williamsburg. "Love rules the court, the camp, the grove," he said—and spoke more prophetically than he knew. For in June 1844, almost two years after the death of Letitia Tyler, and eight months before the end of his term, the widower president took a second wife, Julia Gardiner, in a private ceremony in New York City.

The highlight of the Grant administration's social activity came in 1874 when their idolized daughter, Nellie, wed a young Englishman, Algernon Charles Frederick Sartoris, whom she had met on a trip abroad. The 18-year-old bride, dressed in white satin trimmed with yards of Brussels lace, was married amid elaborate floral decorations in the East Room. The wedding breakfast included an awesome assortment of elegant dishes for the most fashionable event of the season. One participant at the festivities was plainly distraught, however. Tears filled the eyes of President Grant, who was losing his only daughter.

The Grants' son, Fred, a graduate of West Point, married Ida Maria Honore later the same year, though the wedding was not held at the White House. Later the couple came to live with the family, and here a daughter was born and named Julia, after her grandmother.

The wedding of the only president to marry in the White House created a furor in 1886, when 49-year old Grover Cleveland took as his wife lovely 21-year-old Frances Folsom, daughter of his former law partner. The couple planned a private

The Blue Room wedding of President Grover Cleveland to Frances Folsom, in 1886.

wedding; the bridegroom issued fewer than forty handwritten invitations to close friends and relatives. Cleveland had the Blue Room turned into a bower of flowers for the occasion, and church bells all over the city announced the end of the ceremony as a twenty-one-gun salute boomed from the Navy Yard.

Theodore Roosevelt's eldest daughter, Alice—by his first wife, who had died shortly after childbirth—set off social fireworks during the administration.

Right: The wedding party of Jessie Wilson and Francis Bowes Sayre pose in the East Sitting Hall on the Second Floor. President and Mrs. Wilson are in the back row, December 6, 1913.

Left: President Wilson's daughter Eleanor on the day of her marriage to Secretary of the Treasury William Gibbs McAdoo, 1914.

"Princess Alice," as the newspapers called her, became the most headlined debutante and bride of her generation. A thousand guests came to the White House wedding and reception when she married Congressman Nicholas Longworth of Ohio in 1906. Their gifts included rare silks and jade sent by the Empress Dowager of China, a pearl necklace presented by the Cuban government, a feather duster, and a hogshead of popcorn.

President Woodrow Wilson and his first wife, Ellen, launched two of their daughters into marriage in the White House. The wedding of their second daughter, Jessie, to law professor Francis B. Sayre in 1913, was the outstanding social event of the administration, though perhaps not so grandiose as one headline

writer put it: "Nations of all the world do homage to White House bride as she takes solemn vows amid scenes of unequaled splendor." In contrast, the marriage of the Wilson's youngest daughter, Eleanor, to Secretary of the Treasury William Gibbs McAdoo six months later was held to a minimum of display because of the fast-failing health of her mother. In 1915, the widowed president was remarried to Edith Bolling Galt at her Washington home.

More than fifty years later, the weddings of the two daughters of Lyndon and Lady Bird Johnson were highly publicized social events. Scores of reporters, photographers, and television crews recorded Luci's August 1966 church wedding to Patrick J. Nugent of Illinois and the

reception that followed in the flower-adorned mansion. Sixteen months later, in December 1967, Lynda married Captain Charles S. Robb of the U.S. Marine Corps and a former White House social aide, in an elegant East Room ceremony decorated for the Christmas holidays.

Richard and Patricia Nixon's two daughters were also married in the midst of public attention. Julie missed most of the fanfare by marrying David Eisenhower, grandson of the former president, in New York City in 1968, shortly before her father was inaugurated. Tricia, however, chose the White House for her marriage to law student Edward Finch Cox of New York. Arranging for the ceremony to be performed in the famous Rose Garden, on June 12, 1971, she became the first president's daughter to have an outdoor wedding at the White House. Some four hundred guests were seated in the garden, which was decorated with masses of roses, lilies, and petunias. Afterward there was a reception in the mansion. Another family wedding took place in the Rose Garden in May 1994 when Hillary Clinton's brother, Tony Rodham, married Nicolle Boxer.

Above: Former White House bride Alice Roosevelt Longworth greets President Johnson's daughter Lynda and her new husband Charles Robb at their White House wedding in 1967.

Left: President Richard Nixon daughter's Tricia and her husband Edward Cox. Their Rose Garden wedding ceremony was televised in 1971.

Opposite: President Lyndon Johnson's daughter Luci and her attendants on the day of her marriage to Patrick Nugent in August 1966.

Behind the scenes, the men and women who have lived in the Executive Mansion have known the same happiness and frustration, pride, and misery that come to us all. Grief, both national and personal, has been too frequent a caller at the President's House. Eight chief executives have died in office, four of them by assassination.

Every night, the gruff and lonely warrior, Andrew Jackson, performed a tender ritual. After removing the treasured miniature of his dead wife, Rachel, which he carried next to his heart, he would place it on the bedside table near her worn and faded Bible, so that he might see her face first thing on awakening in the morning.

William Henry Harrison was, at 68, the oldest man to become president up to the time of his inauguration in 1841. In an icy wind, he delivered the longest inaugural address in history. Other exposures to wintry weather followed, leading to a cold that turned into pneumonia. One month after his inauguration, he was dead.

During the election year of 1848, Zachary Taylor told supporters that his wife prayed nightly for his defeat. If he were unlucky enough to win the office, she had declared, it would shorten his life. Margaret Taylor's dark prophecy came true a little more than a year after her husband's inauguration. On July 4, 1850, the president sat for hours under the hot sun at a celebration on the grounds of the unfinished Washington Monument. Overheated and exhausted, he became ill of what was then called

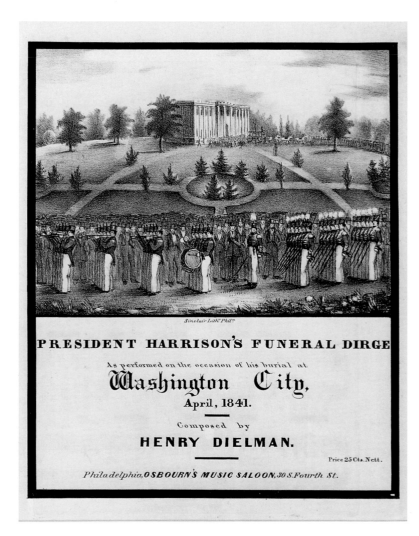

Opposite: The body of President Warren G. Harding lies in state in the East Room of the White House, August 1923.

Above: The Marine Band is pictured in procession on the sheet music for the funeral dirge for President William Henry Harrison, who died one month after his inauguration in 1841.

An engraving depicting a crowd of mourners gathered around the black-draped catafalque in the East Room where President Abraham Lincoln lay in state, April 1865.

cholera morbus — the result, legend would say, of his having consumed too much iced milk and raw cherries. Five days later, Taylor was dead. His grieving widow, secluded in her apartment, could hear the sounds of his office staff making way for the next occupants, and she could feel the vibrations of hammering as workmen assembled a catafalque in the East Room. She could not bear to attend the ceremony, but she was forced to listen to its accom-

paniment, a sympathetic eyewitness reported, "as one band after another blared the funeral music . . . and the heavy guns boomed . . . to announce the final parting."

A devastating blow came to the Lincoln family when son Willie developed a severe fever and died soon afterward, on February 20, 1862. The president shouldered his grief with his other burdens, but high-strung, erratic Mary Lincoln was inconsolable. She turned to spiritualism in the hope of receiving a message from beyond the grave and arranged at least one session with a popular medium of the day at the Soldiers' Home—the Lincolns' "summer White House"—and another in the Red Room. For a while Mrs. Lincoln believed her lost boy had returned. "He comes to me every night," she told her sister, "and stands at the foot of my bed, with the same sweet, adorable smile." Later she wrote, "The loved & idolized being, comes no more." Some insisted that Lincoln himself attended one of the spiritualist meetings, though it was never clear whether this was to please his wife, to satisfy his own curiosity, born of a streak of mysticism, or to show up the medium's tricks.

On the eve of Union victory in early April 1865, Lincoln described a strange dream to his wife and a good friend. In the dream, he said, he was awakened from a deep sleep by a "pitiful sobbing." Getting up, he followed the wailing sound to the East Room, and there he found a catafalque surrounded by mourners. On it he saw a still figure shrouded in funeral garb, the face covered. "The President," one of the soldiers standing in the honor guard whispered to Lincoln, "killed by an assassin." Within two weeks, Abraham Lincoln had been shot by John Wilkes Booth in Ford's Theatre. In the East Room, Lincoln's body lay on a catafalque, surrounded by mourners as foretold by the dream. In her room above, Mary Lincoln lay prostrated by grief. While Tad and Robert sought to comfort her, they could hear the sound of weeping from long lines of people passing the bier to pay their last respects.

In one of the family rooms, frail Eliza Johnson, devoted wife of Andrew Johnson for forty-one years, rocked and sewed as she awaited word of the Senate vote at her husband's impeachment trial in 1868. "I knew he'd be acquitted," she said firmly, but with tears in her eyes, to the official who brought the good news. "I knew it."

For the rest of their lives, Harry and James Garfield would look back in horror upon the morning of July 2, 1881, when they and the president were planning to join his wife, Lucretia, who was then vacationing in Long Branch, New Jersey. The two boys were in high spirits at the prospect of the trip, and President Garfield, a large and active man despite his bookish bent, joined them in a bit of horseplay before they all departed for the Washington depot of the Baltimore and Potomac Railway. Less than an hour later an office-seeking fanatic, Charles Guiteau, fired two shots at Garfield as he entered the waiting room. Garfield fell; physicians rushed to the scene, and a horse-drawn police ambulance soon returned the gravely wounded president to the White House.

For more than two months Garfield battled for life in his Second Floor bedroom at the mansion, while his wife and children waited and prayed. Outside the gates, frequent bulletins kept the public informed of the condition of the man in the sickroom. A metal-detecting device developed by Alexander Graham Bell was

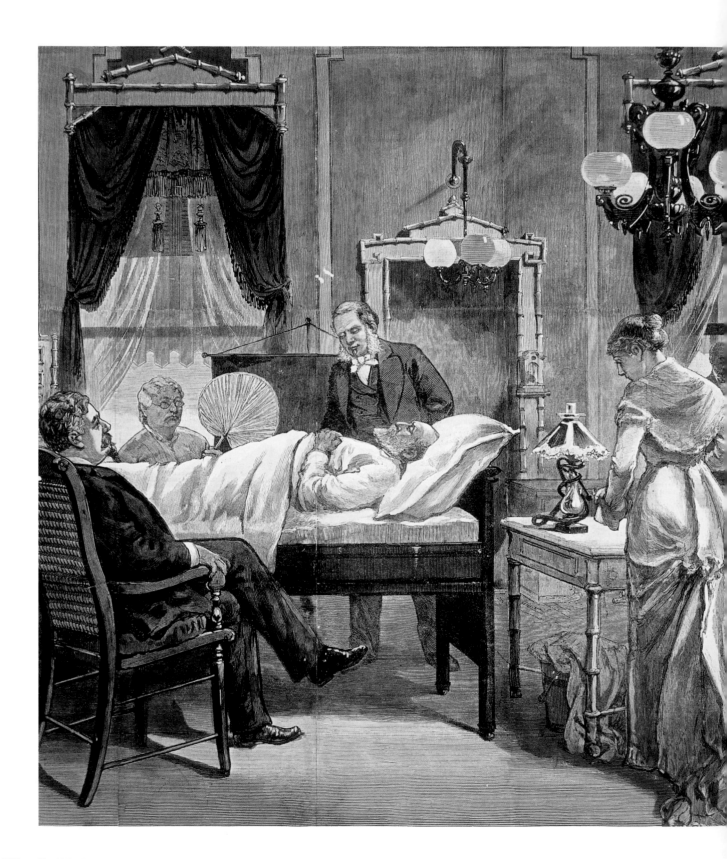

Mortally wounded by an assassin's bullet on July 2, 1881, President James A. Garfield lingered at the White House (opposite) until his death at the New Jersey shore on September 19, 1881. The White House (above) was draped in black in mourning for him, 1881.

used in an attempt to locate the bullet, but the effort failed because of interference from the bed's steel springs. In the hope that sea air might help cure the president, he was transferred by train—with every precaution taken to prevent jolting—to the ocean resort of Elberon at Long Branch. But no air could combat the infection that had developed. Garfield died on September 19, and his body was carried directly to the Capitol to lie in state in the Rotunda. It was the only time in history that a president who had died in office did not lie in state in the East Room.

Fashionable Chester A. Arthur, who succeeded Garfield as president, lived luxuriously in the White House but showed another side of his nature when he was

alone. Like Jackson, he, too, was a recent widower and, like the earlier president, Arthur carried on a ritual of remembrance by ordering fresh roses to be placed daily next to the photograph of his dear Ellen, which was displayed on a little easel. He had been stunned by her sudden death from pneumonia in January 1880, at the age of 42, which left him alone with two children. He demonstrated his love and concern for their young daughter Nellie and their college-age son Alan by keeping them with him as much as possible.

Unlike the murders of Lincoln and Garfield, the third slaying was committed far from Washington. In September 1901, William McKinley was shaking hands with visitors at the Pan-American

GOODBYE ALL, GOODBYE,
IT IS GODS WAY, HIS WILL, NOT OURS BE DONE.

Left: A grieving figure, the stricken nation personified, appears atop William McKinley's mourning ribbon. McKinley was assassinated at the Pan-American Exposition in Buffalo, New York, on September 6, 1901.

Right: A crowd gathers to view the funeral procession of Franklin D. Roosevelt on Pennsylvania Avenue, April 1945.

Exposition in Buffalo, New York, when a young man extended his left hand to the president, then shot him with a concealed revolver. The attack, by an anarchist named Leon Czolgosz, mortally wounded the president. McKinley died eight days later. The courage and strength in adversity of his widow, Ida, would amaze all who had known her as an almost helpless invalid.

Warren G. Harding, on a trip to the western states in the summer of 1923 in the midst of increasing scandals of his administration, died of a heart attack in San Francisco. His body was borne by train back to Washington, where he lay in state in the East Room.

Calvin Coolidge Jr., then barely 16, died in the summer of 1924 — the result of blood poisoning that had developed after he rubbed a blister on his toe while

The body of President Franklin D. Roosevelt lies in state in the East Room, April 14, 1945.

playing tennis on the south grounds of the White House. "When he went," his father wrote in his autobiography, "the power and glory of the Presidency went with him."

One of the most touching scenes in the history of the great changeovers that have come to this house occurred in Eleanor Roosevelt's study on the Second Floor, after the death of her husband. Vice President Harry Truman, summoned to the White House, arrived without knowing of the massive stroke that had ended the president's life at Warm Springs, Georgia. He heard the news from Mrs. Roosevelt. As Truman described the meeting in his memoirs, he asked Mrs. Roosevelt, "Is there anything I can do for

you?" He would never forget her reply, he wrote. "Is there anything we can do for you?" she said. "For you are the one in trouble now."

Sixty-two years after McKinley's death, another assassin pressed a trigger in Dallas. As waves of shock spread from that Texas city, President John F. Kennedy lay dead in the prime of life. Then, once more, the casket of a chief executive rested in the black-draped East Room of the White House. From all over the globe came an extraordinary procession of the world's great — heads of state, prime ministers, and royalty — to pay their last respects and to share the grief of Kennedy's family, friends, and the nation.

A rolling caisson (above), followed by the president's flag, a riderless horse, and an assemblage of world leaders, bears the body of President John F. Kennedy from the White House to St. Matthew's Cathedral on November 25, 1963. The president's family stands on the White House steps (left), preparing to follow his coffin to the cathedral.

SECURITY AND PRIVACY

Today people are not permitted to get as close to the first family as they sometimes did in the past. Nor can individual members of the public enter the White House grounds without an official pass or previous clearance by authorities. Armed, highly trained personnel of the Uniformed Division, U.S. Secret Service, are stationed in gatehouses along the high iron fence and closely check the identity of all callers. The Secret Service maintains various other security measures in carrying out its responsibility of guarding the president—a responsibility given to it in 1901, after William McKinley's assassination. Specific regulations followed; one of the most important requires Secret Service agents to remain near the chief executive at all times. The objective is to offer maximum safeguards with a minimum of interference, but many presidents have grown restive under the attention.

While William H. Taft conceded that the record of assassinations was such that "Congress would be quite derelict" in disregarding it, he added that it was difficult for a chief executive "to avoid the feeling . . . that he was under surveillance rather than under protection." Theodore Roosevelt wrote to a friend: "The secret service men are a very small but very necessary thorn in the flesh." Then he went on to express his belief that no effort could prevent an assault upon his life and quoted Lincoln's remark that "though it would be safer for a President to live in a cage, it would interfere with his business." Since

Opposite: Under the close watch of the Secret Service, tourists gather at the White House fence to catch a glimpse of President Dwight D. Eisenhower.

Above: A Secret Service officer uses binoculars to monitor the activities beyond the North Lawn.

A sentry stands guard at the iron gate near the North Portico during the Civil War.

a 1917 law extended Secret Service protection to other family members, unmarried sons and daughters of presidents have faced the choice of giving up dates or accepting the company—however discreet—of an agent of the Secret Service. John Coolidge's classmates at Amherst joked that John would have to "elope from his agent" if he wanted to marry

anyone. And Margaret Truman, in her book *Souvenir*, gives an account of the "handicap the Secret Service offers to escorts and beaus." She had made up her mind, she wrote, not to marry while she lived in the White House. But she asked the reader "to consider the effect of saying good night to a boy at the door . . . in a blaze of floodlights, with a Secret Service man in attendance. There is not much you can do except shake hands, and that's no way to get engaged."

Subsequent legislation now requires the Secret Service to guard not only the president and his family but also the president-elect, the vice president, their families, as well as former presidents, their widows and minor children, presidential candidates, and top officials from abroad.

Lack of personal privacy is a major concern of presidents and their wives and families, who are never prepared for the intense scrutiny of residents of the White House. Certainly no couple suffered more from it than did the Clevelands. During the election campaign of 1888, scurrilous rumors of Cleveland's mistreatment of his young wife gained such wide circulation that Frances Cleveland issued an indignant denial. "I can wish the women of our Country no greater blessing," she said, "than that their homes and lives may be as happy, and their husbands may be as kind, attentive, considerate and affectionate as mine."

Despite whatever hazards and lack of privacy our modern presidents may endure, nothing could approach the conditions that prevailed in family living arrangements until the beginning of the twentieth century. Until Theodore Roosevelt moved to new offices in the West Wing, the executive offices and family apartment shared space in the mansion itself. For much of the time, these rooms occupied opposite ends of the same floor.

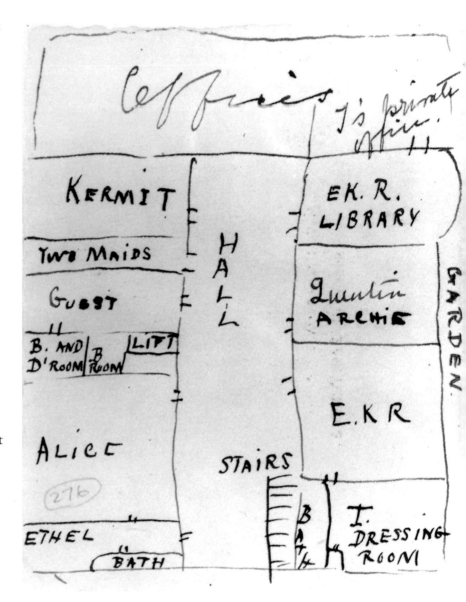

This sketch made by First Lady Edith Roosevelt in 1901 shows the close proximity of the first family's crowded private quarters to the office spaces of the White House.

In those days, a multitude of callers, ranging from tradesmen and patronage-seekers to cabinet officers and foreign dignitaries, streamed into and out of the north entrance. Some lounged as they waited in rooms on the State Floor; others trudged up the public stairway to see the president or members of his staff. To avoid the often-rough crowds, some of the

older and more delicate wives of presidents seldom ventured out of their west-side family quarters.

One of these was the First Lady Letitia Tyler. An invalid from a stroke suffered before she came to the White House, she managed to run the household from her bedroom. This she did so efficiently and "so quietly," wrote her admiring daughter-in-law, Priscilla, "that you can't tell when she does it."

Margaret Taylor was a reluctant first lady and a White House homebody. She received visitors only in her own quarters and limited her guests almost entirely to close friends and to relatives from the South. The general, she felt, deserved a rest after forty years of active duty that

included service in the War of 1812, in skirmishes with frontier Indians, and in the Mexican War.

In later administrations, as executive responsibilities grew heavier and the number of visitors increased, presidential families faced ever-greater inconveniences. A member of President Garfield's staff recalled in his memoirs that a mere acquaintance of the family "pushed himself in past the doors that marked the private domain . . . and took his afternoon siesta upon the most comfortable sofa he could find."

Caroline Harrison, wife of President Benjamin Harrison, in an 1889 interview, complained that she was "being made a circus of. . . . I've been a show, the whole

family's been a show since Mr. Harrison was elected," she said. "All last fall I sat in my sewing room and watched the procession of feet pass across the parlor floor wearing their path into the nap, and disappear like the trail of a caravan into the General's room beyond. Day by day, I watched the path grow wider and deeper. . . . But I don't propose to be made a circus of forever! If there's any privacy to be found in the White House, I propose to find it."

Mrs. Harrison's solution to the problem called for Congress to adopt one of three drastic measures, for which she presented detailed architectural plans. The simplest of these would have provided the president with a separate residence and remodeled the mansion for entertaining and executive business only. The second design proposed the addition of wings to be used for office and guest suites. The most elaborate of the suggestions was to extend the house into a fantastic four-sided palace enclosing a huge court and fountains. Though Congress rejected Mrs. Harrison's projects, it did appropriate $35,000 for essential housecleaning and repairs to the deteriorating old house. Moreover, airing the need for reasonable family privacy and adequate office space helped pave the way for the future construction of wings on the west and east sides of the mansion to serve as offices and for service functions.

President and Mrs. George W. Bush are surrounded by Secret Service protection as they walk down Pennsylvania Avenue in his second inaugural parade, 2005.

Making and Furnishing a Home

From the beginning, each president and his family have created a highly individual home within the Executive Mansion by furnishing and embellishing it in their own taste. The White House occupies a unique place in American life. As the home of presidential families for more than two hundred years, it has represented, by democratic extension, the homes and families of all Americans. "I was always conscious of the character which a century of history had impressed upon the White House," wrote Helen Taft, but "it came . . . to feel as much like home as any house I have ever occupied." Similar thoughts were expressed by Grace Coolidge, who saw the house as a home "rich in tradition, mellow with years, hallowed with memories." The personal and family life in the White House has given to this center of national

Frances Folsom Cleveland
sits by the fire, c. 1893.

power and influence a warm, human note of common experience and understanding.

Since the early Federal period of John and Abigail Adams, this "First Home" has mirrored America's everyday domestic fashions and attitudes, household decor, furnishings and tableware, in ways that would have been unthinkable to the followers of social and political traditions practiced in Europe's great state residences. Beginning with John Adams, whose personal discomfort in the new White House was matched only by the political vicissitudes of his outgoing administration, each succeeding president has led two lives while in office—his own and his country's.

President and Mrs. John Adams, for instance, were apprehensive in November 1800 when the time came to move into the damp and incomplete Executive Mansion being readied in the new capital city. Only four months remained of Adams's single term, and Mrs. Adams was dismayed at the condition of their temporary home and its grounds. The most famous housekeeping problem Mrs. Adams faced still makes an amusing subject for conversation at White House parties. Since there was, she said, "not the least fence, yard, or other convenience" available outside, she had a servant hang the presidential laundry to dry in the huge, unfinished East Room, destined to become the most elegant of the State Rooms used for entertaining.

Thomas Jefferson maintained an atmosphere of personal moderation and intellectual interests that belied the crude surroundings of the wilderness capital. To

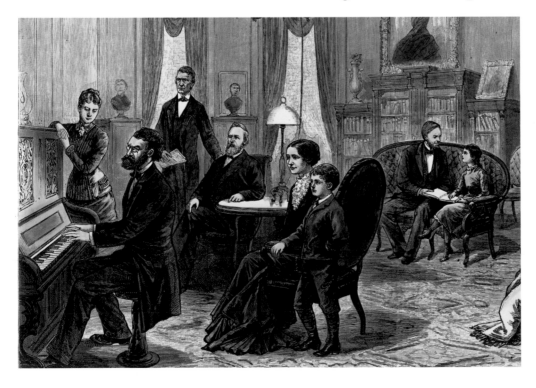

President Rutherford B. Hayes and his family often gathered with cabinet members in the Second Floor family library to sing hymns on Sunday nights, c. 1880.

relax from the heavy responsibilities of leadership in a young republic starting out in a world of hostile monarchies, the long-widowed president turned to hobbies he had enjoyed at his Monticello home. He played his violin, experimented with familiar and rare plants, and taught his pet mockingbird to peck food from his lips and to hop up the stairs after him.

The White House reflected the quiet happiness of James and Dolley Madison and the generous hospitality presided over by the genial Dolley before they were burned out of the mansion in the War of 1812. Observers praised the couple's mutual admiration. Dolley Madison expressed her warm and vibrant personality in decorating her parlor (today's Red Room) with bright yellow draperies and upholstery.

Abigail Fillmore, a onetime schoolteacher, had met her husband-to-be when they attended school together. She obtained congressional funds for the first official library in the Executive Mansion. With a dictionary, histories, sets of Charles Dickens, William Makepeace Thackeray, and other works, she filled the bookshelves installed in the upstairs oval sitting room. There she and President Millard Fillmore spent many quiet evenings reading and chatting, while their young daughter, Mary Abigail, played the piano or harp.

Sedate and proper Lucy Hayes had her bedroom walls "tinted pale blue, with panels of light gray and pink," as described by a woman correspondent permitted the rare privilege of seeing the Hayeses' private apartment in the 1870s.

Presidential families have the option of bringing their own furnishings and personal belongings to the residence, and personal possessions have moved in and out of the White House with each successive family. With the Tafts, for instance, came the president's many law books, recalling his long and distinguished legal career capped eventually by his appointment as chief justice of the United States. The

Cartoonist Clifford Berryman depicts a Teddy Bear deciding whether to leave the White House with President Theodore Roosevelt's possessions on moving day in March 1909.

TO GO OR NOT TO GO?   March 2, 1909.

erudite Hoovers brought many mementos from their world travels: South American rugs, Asian art, caged songbirds, and books in various languages, including their own translation from Latin of an important sixteenth-century volume on mining. All helped Lou Hoover transform the broad, bare hall on the Second Floor into an inviting reception area for guests.

To the White House from Hyde Park, New York, Franklin and Eleanor Roosevelt shipped a wheelchair to carry the president along the family corridor. They also brought sturdy handcrafted furniture that had been scratched during family pillow fights and wrestling matches in which "Pa," with his powerful shoulders, won as often as his sons. When Mrs. Roosevelt left the White House in 1945 after the death of the president, twelve years of accumulation required twenty big army trucks to transport the possessions back to Hyde Park.

Every president's family takes its place in the flow of historic continuity, finding

A moving van parked at the South Portico delivers President and Mrs. Clinton's possessions to the White House on January 20, 1993.

its own uses for the many public and private spaces within the various levels of the White House. Before Theodore Roosevelt separated his office from his home, the basement of the mansion — now called the Ground Floor — served as a service and storage area, cluttered with buckets and lumber and defaced with pipes run through the walls. Today, this wide corridor shows off nineteenth-century American furnishings and displays on its walls a gallery of first ladies' portraits, an idea first suggested by Edith Roosevelt in 1902. Off the corridor are several handsome rooms, including the Library, with its nineteenth-century portraits of Native Americans; the China Room, showcasing the varied presidential table services; and the Map Room, where FDR kept up with World War II's progress.

During the Trumans' time, the Second Floor held three pianos — appropriate symbols of the harmony that characterized the spunky, close-knit family from Independence, Missouri. One piano stood in the oval room that was then the president's study; daughter Margaret practiced on another in her sitting room, where she also kept her record collection; while a third — a spinet in the hall — was frequently used for duets. The Truman family often spent evenings together, reading, playing, or listening to music.

A few years later, when friends of President Eisenhower visited him in the upstairs oval room, which he, too, used as a study, they found displayed there a fascinating array of military and civilian awards, decorations, swords, and other gifts presented by world leaders. In his book *The White House Years,* the president wrote that he received visitors in the study "informally in the evening, whenever a somewhat homier atmosphere than could be obtained in my office was desirable." His "personal mementos of a fairly long life," he added, "were kept there for a temporary period only, and later were transferred to a suitable museum — the Smithsonian, the Library of Congress, or the museum which bears my name in Abilene, Kansas." For the Eisenhowers, the White House was the most permanent home they had known during the far-ranging career of the popular army general. "I have seen my grandchildren growing up in these historic rooms," Mamie Eisenhower wrote. "Here

Opposite: In preparation for the Nixon family's move into the White House, Lady Bird Johnson reviews floor plans with incoming First Lady Pat Nixon and Chief Usher J. B. West in the West Sitting Hall, in November 1968.

Below: President Dwight Eisenhower enjoyed barbequing outside the Third Floor Solarium.

President Jimmy Carter's family during a meal in the President's Dining Room on the Second Floor.

my son and daughter-in-law have shared our family evenings."

The changing scenes on the family floor continued to mirror, in colors and furnishings, the tastes and activities of each new group of White House occupants. Mrs. Eisenhower's decor, with its "Mamie pink" accents, gave way to Mrs. Kennedy's light blue curtains and blue-and-white furnishings that showed to advantage against plain off-white walls in the private bedroom and sitting room areas. American period pieces, French antiques, and valuable art objects began to appear in various places: the sitting halls that share the wide corridor; the Queens' and Lincoln Bedrooms, where visiting royalty had slept; and what was called the

Treaty Room, then decorated in Victorian style. They gave visible evidence of Jacqueline Kennedy's program to restore to the White House furnishings that awaken a feeling of the historic past of the nation and the house.

The Yellow Oval Room on the Second Floor has served the same function for the last nine administrations. Mrs. Kennedy turned this room into a formal drawing room, and it has proved to be the most suitable place in the house to entertain state guests before dinners or luncheons given in their honor. Many families have placed their family Christmas tree here, where the first White House Christmas tree was displayed in 1889. With the arrival of the Johnson family, Lady Bird

Johnson put her own signature on the look and use of the Second Floor apartments. In her mainly green-and-yellow bedroom, she set up a cozy working space in which she dictated letters and speeches, and planned and directed her many activities. Down the hall—in rooms that had lately known the toys of the Kennedy children—the Johnsons' teenage girls, Lynda and Luci, had their bedrooms until marriage took them both to homes of their own. And when Richard Nixon brought his family to the White House in 1969, his daughter Tricia moved into the suite that had been used by Lynda and Luci. After the Carters moved in, 10-year-old Amy occupied the bedroom that had been Luci Johnson's, then Tricia Nixon's.

Life for President Jimmy Carter and his family reflected the easy atmosphere found in many small southern towns, such as their native Plains, Georgia. A story that made the capital rounds early in 1977 revealed something of their ways. Picking up a telephone soon after she arrived at the White House, Rosalynn Carter asked to be connected with Jimmy. "Jimmy who?" came the response from the operator.

Ronald and Nancy Reagan put their California-inspired stamp on the Second Floor family quarters, as well as on the expanded living space that was added as the Third Floor in 1927, during the Coolidge administration. Most of this floor was then divided into bedroom, bath, and sitting room apartments, which are available today for family members and personal guests. The remaining areas serve as space for storage and housekeeping.

The George H. W. Bushes created a warm family atmosphere in the White House. Family photographs were displayed throughout the private quarters, and stuffed toys were available for their grandchildren when they visited. The focal point of the family sitting room was a needlepoint rug with floral and animal motifs that Barbara Bush had worked on for many years.

Hillary and Bill Clinton instituted a casual life for their family, sharing family meals with their daughter in the Second Floor kitchen. On the Third Floor, a special music room for the president, with instruments and memorabilia, was created for him as a gift from Mrs. Clinton.

The White House has an extensive collection of furniture and art that reflects

President and Mrs. Reagan often dined off tray tables in the private quarters while watching the evening news, 1981.

the changing styles of the times and the personalities of its inhabitants. Each first lady may make selections from furniture

First Lady Jacqueline Kennedy's portrait hangs in the Vermeil Room (pictured above) following its refurbishment in 2006. Changes to the decor of this and other public rooms on the State Floor and the Ground Floor are approved by the Committee for the Preservation of the White House, established in 1964.

already in the mansion or from an off-site support facility containing pieces used by previous residents. And, of course, she may refurnish and redecorate the Second and Third Floor quarters as she chooses. The Ground Floor Corridor and principal public rooms on the State Floor, however, retain their museum character, in accordance with a law passed by Congress in 1961 to protect and continue the historical work begun by Jacqueline Kennedy. Major changes in these rooms must now be approved by the Committee for the Preservation of the White House, established in 1964 by executive order.

Before George W. and Laura Bush arrived at the White House, Mrs. Bush called her mother-in-law, Barbara Bush, to ask her what she should bring. "She told me there were already so many lovely and comfortable furnishings in the White

House that we would need to bring very little." George W. Bush, like his father and many presidents before him, uses as his private office a Second Floor room where presidents in the late nineteenth century convened their cabinet meetings. In 1962 Mrs. Kennedy redecorated this room with furnishings from the Cabinet Room of Ulysses S. Grant, and it was renamed the Treaty Room, in commemoration of the many historic documents signed there.

The impressive Victorian walnut table that serves as a desk for President Bush was ordered by Ulysses S. Grant and has eight locking drawers—enough for Grant and each member of his cabinet. Jimmy Carter had this table placed on the north grounds for the signing of the treaty between Egypt and Israel in March 1979. Then in September 1993, William J. Clinton had it moved to the South Lawn for the signing of the peace accord between the Israelis and the Palestine Liberation Organization, and again on July 25, 1994, for the declaration ending the state of war between Jordan and Israel.

Two paintings add to the historical character of the room: a large painting of President William McKinley at the signing of the protocol ending the war against Spain in 1898, and a painting by G.P.A. Healy entitled *The Peacemakers*, which depicts Abraham Lincoln conferring with three of his military leaders about the prospect of peace at the conclusion of the Civil War.

In part because of the enormous responsibilities and stresses that are

Left: First Lady Barbara
Bush with a new grand-
child, Charles Walker
Bush, 1989.

Below: President Bill
Clinton practices the
saxophone in his
Music Room, 1995.

President George W. Bush at work in his residence office, the Treaty Room, c. 2001.

inherent in the presidency, Laura Bush has tried to create a sense of serenity and comfort in the residence. "I want this to be a warm, relaxing place to come at the end of the day," she says. For this reason, she has enjoyed working with the sunny yellows that were already there and adding soft, muted greens. "And as a lifelong gardener, one of my greatest pleasures each day is the abundance of beautiful flowers throughout this home."

The floral preferences of first ladies make a varied bouquet. Mamie Eisenhower, for example, showed a preference for sweetheart roses and carnations in her favorite color, pink. Jacqueline Kennedy experimented with mixed floral designs, and Lady Bird Johnson enjoyed each season's offerings — from spring pastels to deeper shades of fall. Pat Nixon took keen interest in planning floral colors and

designs for State Dinners. Betty Ford showed a definite preference for all kinds of lilies. Rosalynn Carter's choices followed the Kennedy style with simple garden flowers, such as roses and daisies. Nancy Reagan loved peonies and coral-colored arrangements in vermeil bowls. Barbara Bush, who was an avid gardener, was especially fond of peonies, lilies, and all varieties of summer flowers. Hillary Clinton favored contemporary arrangements of warm-colored red and yellow flowers, as well as those using a variety of garden flowers. Laura Bush delights in the fresh flowers, especially roses and tulips, that grace the public rooms on the State Floor and the private living quarters in the White House. Floral arrangements are prepared by chief White House floral designer Nancy Clarke, and her talented staff.

Left: First Lady Rosalynn Carter, pictured with Joan Mondale, wife of the vice president, works on a flower arrangement in the Solarium on the Third Floor of the White House.

Below: Nancy Clarke prepares daisies for placement at the congressional picnic during the George W. Bush administration, 2006.

In the President's Park

4

Few settings are lovelier than the rolling expanse of lawn to the south of the White House. Looking past a shimmering pool and fountains toward the Washington Monument and Jefferson Memorial, one would not suspect that the lawn once merged with malarial marshes along a creek, which by 1817 had been walled and deepened into a sluggish canal. Odorous with sewage and dead animals, alive with mosquitoes and flies, the canal was the bane of White House occupants. As a summer retreat, Martin Van Buren rented a house north of nearby Georgetown. Later presidents, including Abraham Lincoln and Rutherford B. Hayes, were glad to go in the hot months to a cottage at the Soldiers' Home, three miles away. "I am alone in the White pest-house," a Lincoln secretary wrote a friend. "The ghosts of twenty thousand drowned cats come in at night through the south windows." In 1872 the canal-sewer was covered and the street above it named Constitution Avenue. With landscaping, the present Ellipse was completed by 1884.

Today the President's Park, with its well-kept gardens and grounds, is open to the public in the spring and fall, continuing a tradition begun by Patricia Nixon in 1972. Visitors view the Rose Garden, the Jacqueline Kennedy Garden, and the Children's Garden, and they admire the expansive south grounds. In 2005 Laura Bush added four summer tours.

Guests stroll on the South Lawn of the White House during a garden party hosted by President and Mrs. Theodore Roosevelt, c. 1901–9.

The Grounds and the Gardens

Over the years, the 18-acre estate that today surrounds the White House has shown many different faces. John and Abigail Adams found it a barren expanse littered with workmen's shacks and tools. The grounds had appeared so grim before their arrival, in fact, that a member of the president's cabinet wrote to one of the District Commissioners complaining that "a private gentleman preparing a residence for his Friend, would have done more than has been done." He suggested that the Commissioners plant "something like a

The President's House, probably drawn by Benjamin Henry Latrobe, in 1811, showing the north front, or public side of the house.

The White House and
Capitol in about 1827
during John Quincy
Adams's presidency.
President Jefferson's
stone wall, open pas-
tures, and the orchard
and vegetable garden
can be seen in this
view of the southwest
side of the house.

garden, at the North side of . . . [the] large, naked, ugly looking building" and provide a yard enclosure.

Thomas Jefferson obtained funds to build the first fence. For a few years, this rustic rail-and-post enclosure blended nicely into a village capital where "excellent snipe shooting and even partridge shooting was to be had on either side of the main avenue," as the secretary of the British Legation noted. Then Jefferson replaced the wood fence with a fieldstone wall and constructed an imposing arched gate, designed by architect Benjamin Henry Latrobe, over the driveway leading to the southeast entrance. Jefferson also devised an overall landscape plan that included grading and planting the south grounds to provide more privacy, while leaving a central view toward the river.

It remained, however, for that austere New Englander and ardent gardener, John Quincy Adams, to devote the most lavish personal care of any president to the White House nurseries and gardens. His diaries from 1825 to 1829 tell of the happy hours he spent on this hobby. Entries reveal his enjoyment of pungent herbs—balm, rue, sage, tansy, and tarragon—and his delight in the "deep blood-colored beet, the white-flowered carrot and yellow-flowered parsnip." In this "small garden, of less than two acres," he wrote, there were "forest- and fruit-trees, shrubs, hedges, esculent vegetables, kitchen and medicinal herbs, hot-house plants, flowers and weeds, to the amount, I conjecture, of at least one thousand."

Adams planned to introduce useful crops to American farmers. On his rides

about Washington and on travels to and
from his Massachusetts home, he collected
nuts, seeds, and seedlings, and he encouraged his friends to do the same when they
went abroad. After Congress passed a res-
olution to encourage the growing of mulberry trees to form a base for a silkworm
industry in the United States, Adams
added the white mulberry to his flourish-
ing White House nurseries. With his wife,
Louisa, he nurtured silkworms on the
leaves, and in the evenings he would sit
beside her, writing, as she unreeled and

rewound the fragile silk filaments from the
cocoons. Adams's dream of a silk industry
in America never materialized.

With the arrival of Andrew Jackson
and the building of the North Portico
that completed construction of the mansion, the evolution of the grounds entered
a new phase. Instead of the rambling
gardens of Adams, graveled footways
appeared, along with a carriage house,
driveway, stable for the president's
favorite racing horses, and an orangery
on the east side. As Washington grew less

bucolic, the President's Park was enhanced with fountains and flower beds. In 1842, when Charles Dickens called to see President John Tyler, he found the "ornamental ground about it . . . laid out in garden walks; they are pretty and agreeable to the eye; though they have that uncomfortable air of having been made yesterday."

Time and professional landscape architects, including the talented Andrew Jackson Downing, would overcome the effect of newness that Dickens observed.

Within fifteen years, the White House estate, particularly its tree-dotted South Lawn, had become part of "a scene of beauty and attractiveness," according to an article in an 1856 issue of *United States Magazine*. Open to the public on weekdays, the "agreeable promenades" drew "the elite of the city," said the author. "Usually the President, the Cabinet, and the Foreign Ministers and their wives may be seen here [with] thousands of ladies and pretty children, most bewitchingly dressed."

Visitors stroll on the south grounds of the White House, c. 1857.

THE ROSE GARDEN

Adjacent to the South Lawn and just outside the Oval Office, the Rose Garden has long been a favorite of presidents. Ellen Wilson planted the first roses here in 1913, replacing a colonial style garden dating from 1902. In 1962, at the request of John Kennedy, Rachel Lambert Mellon supervised its redesign by the landscape architect Perry Wheeler. The garden's broad lawn, seasonal flower beds, and saucer magnolia and crab apple trees provide a serene setting for the president as he walks to the Oval Office or looks out from his office. They are also an attractive stage for official ceremonies such as bill signings, press conferences,

President Herbert Hoover speaking at an event near the Rose Garden, c. 1932.

presidential announcements, and elegant dinners.

Here President Kennedy greeted the early astronauts, and here, in 1971, Tricia Nixon was married. During the Bicentennial year, 1976, Gerald and Betty Ford hosted several State Dinners under a large tent covering the garden, including one for Queen Elizabeth II of Great Britain. In a ceremony on September 24, 1981, Ronald Reagan honored Sandra Day O'Connor—the first woman to be named to the U.S. Supreme Court. George H. W. Bush also held numerous official events in the Rose Garden, including a meeting with the Cincinnati Reds after their victory in the 1990 World Series. William J. Clinton held several press conferences in the garden, and it was here that he signed such historic legislation as the Family Leave Act in 1993.

President George W. Bush also frequently uses the Rose Garden. Here he has presented Teacher of the Year and Preserve America awards, announced major policy initiatives such as Medicare drug plan, Homeland Security, and trade agreements, and greeted several championship athletic teams. In 2005 he and First Lady Laura Bush hosted a special Cinco de Mayo dinner in the Rose Garden, under festive lights.

President John F. Kennedy meets with Peace Corps volunteers in the Rose Garden, 1961.

A bird's-eye view of a dinner held by President and Mrs. George W. Bush in the Rose Garden in celebration of Cinco de Mayo, 2005.

The Jacqueline Kennedy Garden

Variously named the East Garden and the First Lady's Garden, this intimate, quiet setting on the east side of the White House has always been a private garden and retreat for first families and their friends. In 1903, Edith Roosevelt, who had a strong interest in gardening, created a formal garden where, at spring garden parties, guests walked along the graveled paths to view the flower beds of roses and lilies outlined with boxwood and privet. Ten years later, another first lady with a love of gardens, Ellen Wilson, invited the

A view of the Jacqueline Kennedy Garden looking toward the South Portico, during an event hosted by President and Mrs. George W. Bush, 2003.

highly respected landscape gardener Beatrix Jones Farrand to submit plans for the garden. The result was an expansive central green lawn with a lily pond in the center, surrounded by ivy plantings, evergreens, and four L-shaped flower beds in the corners. Changes made in 1952, at the end of the massive Truman renovation of the house, simplified the garden.

Shortly after moving into the White House in 1963, Lady Bird Johnson asked that the plans for the garden, begun by Rachel Lambert Mellon and approved by President John and First Lady Jacqueline Kennedy and the National Park Service, be continued. The plan retained a central grass panel in the center with the north and south sides framed by holly osmanthus hedges and square planting beds with clipped American holly trees. Also in the beds are herbs grown for the White House chefs. When Mrs. Johnson dedicated the garden to Mrs. Kennedy in 1965 she stated, "I dedicate it to the enduring heritage she has given all of us."

Succeeding first ladies have held receptions and teas in this serene setting and, in the 1990s, Hillary Rodham Clinton showcased eight exhibitions of American contemporary sculpture in the garden, organized by museums throughout the country. George W. and Laura Bush have hosted receptions in the garden before large events held elsewhere in the complex. Guests invited to watch a film in the newly renovated movie theater, housed in the nearby east terrace, have also enjoyed receptions in the garden.

George Segal's *Walking Man* (foreground) and Richard Hunt's *Farmer's Dream* were included in the first of eight exhibitions of contemporary sculpture initiated by First Lady Hillary Rodham Clinton, 1994–95.

GREENHOUSES

President James Buchanan's niece and official hostess, Harriet Lane, persuaded her uncle to build the first of several conservatories and greenhouses that would give much pleasure to future White House residents and visitors. In these steamy glass buildings, filled with the color and fragrance of exotic blossoms, fruits, and tangled tropical vines, Miss Lane became the first of many hostesses at the mansion to find a quiet haven away from the obligations of her official position.

The energetic first lady Lucy Hayes worked here with trowel and shears among her lilies and roses. Frances Cleveland spent pleasant hours wandering with her girls along the sweet-scented aisles of the greenhouses. Caroline Harrison, who was fond of orchids, had several rare varieties planted in the conservatory, and she used the vivid, showy blooms as models for china she selected and painted.

From the time President Buchanan's conservatory opened until all the "glass houses" were torn down to make way for the West Wing in 1902 during the administration of Theodore Roosevelt, no first lady had far to go for flowers or potted plants to decorate her home. Today, all flowers for arrangements come from wholesale distributors. Off-site greenhouses run by the National Park Service, which is responsible for the care and upkeep of the grounds, supply potted plants and azaleas, roses, hydrangeas, and orchids.

Opposite: First Lady Lucy Webb Hayes and her children Fanny and Scott, with their playmate, in the greenhouse, c. 1879.

Below: The White House conservatories as they appeared in the late nineteenth century, where the West Wing stands today.

The Children's Garden

Created in 1969 at the request of Lyndon and Lady Bird Johnson as a private place for children and grandchildren of presidential families, this garden on the south grounds is a quiet, secluded spot. With its child-size garden furniture, small pool, and flagstone blocks with handprints of recent presidential children and grandchildren, it evokes the memory of all children who have resided at the White House.

Children have found the rolling acres of the South Lawn a great playground. Here they can explore hidden nooks in hedges and bushes, ride ponies, and raise pets of every description. Little Tad Lincoln made a pet of a turkey that relatives sent for the family's Christmas dinner in 1863. He named it Jack. When the cook prepared to kill the turkey, Tad ran in tears to his father, who interrupted a cabinet meeting to write an official reprieve. The event became immortalized in the president's "pardoning" of a Thanksgiving turkey each year. In 2006 George W. Bush "pardoned" a turkey presented by the National Turkey Federation, marking the fifty-ninth consecutive pardoning.

Another president's son faced a less amenable father. TR once caught young Quentin walking on stilts through a flower bed. The boy obeyed Roosevelt's stern order to get out of the flowers but grumbled, "I don't see what good it does me for you to be President."

Caroline Kennedy's pony was stabled on the far south grounds, while a playground for her and her young brother, John, was closer to the house.

Handprints of children from recent first families line the path in the Children's Garden, 2003.

Left: President Dwight Eisenhower offers a cranberry to a turkey during the annual presidential turkey pardoning ceremony, 1954.

Below left: Macaroni and the Kennedy children visit the president outside the Oval Office, 1962.

Below right: President Jimmy Carter is seen with daughter Amy and a grandchild playing in the treehouse he designed for them on the south grounds, c. 1977.

COMMEMORATIVE TREES

Above: Children look on as First Lady Lady Bird Johnson plants a tree on the White House grounds in 1968.

Right: In 1977, President and Mrs. Jimmy Carter plant a red maple tree, near the North Portico.

John Quincy Adams indulged in the hope, he confided to his diary, that a certain border of oaks, chestnuts, and other trees would "outlast many Presidents of the United States." In fact one of his shade trees—a great American elm—survived until 1990, spreading its branches over the southeast lawn. In its place, Barbara Bush planted a new tree in 1991, one that had been propagated from the Adams elm.

Andrew Jackson was one of the first presidents to plant a memorial tree on the grounds, a magnificent magnolia in memory of his beloved Rachel. It still stands beside the South Portico.

Beginning with Rutherford B. Hayes, all the presidents and some of their wives have planted trees in the President's Park. Jimmy Carter brought a red maple from his Georgia farm. He knew all the old trees by name and took a special interest in their care. Ronald Reagan planted

three trees, the George H. W. Bushes, five. Bill and Hillary Clinton added more than half a dozen to the park, including a white dogwood planted in memory of the children who died in the April 1995 bombing of the federal building in Oklahoma City.

George W. and Laura Bush have planted a silver maple tree to replace an older, deteriorating maple and a little leaf linden on the south grounds, and in 2005 an American chestnut was planted on the north grounds. By planting these trees the Bushes were following the Olmsted Plan of 1935, which ensures that the grounds of the White House are historically maintained according to the plan accepted in the days of the Roosevelts. The Bushes have also planted a bright purple petunia named in honor of Laura Bush around the pool and South Portico.

Above: President and Mrs. Bill Clinton plant a dogwood tree in memory of the Oklahoma City bombing victims, 1995.

Left: President and Mrs. George W. Bush plant an elm tree on the North Lawn of the White House on October 2, 2006. The new tree replaced a 150-year-old American elm—depicted on the back of the $20 bill—that was destroyed in a heavy storm in June 2006.

Events on the Lawns

From the beginning, the White House gardens and lawns have been settings for pageantry, entertainment, and the recreation of presidents. Thomas Jefferson's Fourth of July celebrations included reviews of the District of Columbia militia and other troops in the newly laid out "President's Park," with "their gay appearance and martial musick," wrote an eyewitness, "enlivening the scene, exhilarating the spirits of the throngs of people who poured in from the country and adjacent towns." In the mid-nineteenth century, several administrations invited Washingtonians to Marine Band concerts on the South Lawn on Saturday afternoons.

Opposite: President Franklin Roosevelt gives his inaugural speech from the South Portico of the White House, 1945. The general public, servicemen and the press can be seen in the crowd of onlookers.

Below: President Abraham Lincoln towers over his guest Prince Napoleon on the South Portico, July 21, 1861. Beyond the flag crowned Marine Band pavilion, the unfinished Washington Monument rises.

From the 1870s to the 1930s, large lawn parties regularly complemented the Marine Band concerts, with the band seated on the South Portico. In the summer of 1918, Woodrow and Edith Wilson invited war veterans to attend an annual garden fete. Warren and Florence Harding continued these parties for veterans with much enthusiasm.

When the Tafts celebrated their silver wedding anniversary in June 1911, they received more than three thousand guests on the south grounds, where trees and bushes sparkled with tiny colored lights and strings of paper lanterns cast shadows on the lawn. Helen Taft later wrote happily of the occasion that "a more brilliant throng was never gathered in this country." That same year the broad south grounds witnessed a prophetic and dramatic sight. A pioneering pilot, Harry Nelson Atwood, landed there in a Burgess-Wright biplane soon after completing a record-setting cross-country flight, and President Taft presented him with a gold medal for the feat.

On a cold day in January 1945, hundreds of guests (many were members of the armed forces) stood on the South Lawn to witness the fourth inauguration of President Franklin D. Roosevelt on the South Portico. It was the only inauguration to be held outdoors at the White House.

Summer after summer, the South Lawn has offered a perfect setting for large gatherings. The Eisenhowers, for example, held a reception there for more than four thousand members of the American Bar Association and counselors from the British Commonwealth. The Kennedy children shared their playground with 1,700 youngsters from child-care agencies when the kilted Black Watch—the Royal Highland Regiment—paraded to the skirl of bagpipes. On a huge stage erected for the occasion, Lyndon Johnson presented awards to outstanding high school graduates who had won a place in his annual Presidential-Scholar program, begun in 1964. Here George H. W. Bush signed the Americans with Disabilities Act before a large crowd. Here William J. Clinton hosted the largest gathering of American Indian tribal leaders to congregate at the White House and a dinner commemorating the fiftieth anniversary of North Atlantic Treaty Organization, attended by several hundred leaders of NATO countries.

The South Lawn served as the backdrop for the arrival of the 2002 Olympic torch in Washington as it made its way to Salt Lake City, Utah, and as the setting for welcoming United States Olympic athletes at the end of the 2002 and 2004 games. On the lawn in September 2005, George W. Bush awarded the 9/11 Medals of Valor in honor of the 442 firefighters, police officers, emergency medical technicians, and other public safety officers who gave their lives on September 11, 2001.

Each summer, continuing a tradition started by Lyndon Johnson, George W. and Laura Bush host the annual picnic on the South Lawn for members of Congress and their families. At the 2005 picnic, an

Left: President George H. W. Bush signs into law the Americans with Disabilities Act on the South Lawn of the White House, 1990.

Below left: A scene from a tee-ball game on the South Lawn, 2006.

Below right: Children at a congressional picnic watch a cowboy perform, 2006.

A ceremony on the North Lawn of the White House for the signing of the Egypt-Israel Peace Treaty in 1979. Seated at the table are Egyptian President Anwar al-Sadat, President Jimmy Carter, and Israeli Prime Minister Menahem Begin.

"In Performance at the White House" concert featuring Tom Wopat, Harolyn Blackwell, Shirley Jones, and Cartier Williams entertained the guests with Broadway hits. The South Lawn also is the setting for ceremonial occasions, such as the welcoming of a head of state for a state visit. In 1993, in an event orchestrated by President Clinton, thousands gathered to witness the emotional signing of the Israeli-Palestinian peace agreement. During the George W. Bush administration, moments of prayer and remembrance have been observed for victims of the 2001 terrorist attacks and their families.

On April 10, 1865, jubilant crowds surged across the North Lawn, singing and cheering over the news of General Robert E. Lee's surrender at Appomattox Court House. Soon Abraham Lincoln came to a window in response to the cries of the people. He promised a victory speech later but meantime suggested that their enthusiastic band play "Dixie." It was one of the best tunes he had ever heard, he said, and he thought "we had fairly captured it."

Only a few ceremonies have been held on the North Lawn facing toward Pennsylvania Avenue. One that received worldwide attention was the 1979 signing of the Treaty of Peace between Prime Minister Menahem Begin of Israel and President Anwar al-Sadat of Egypt, which

President Jimmy Carter had negotiated. That same year, President and Mrs. Carter welcomed Pope John Paul II, the first pontiff to meet with a president at the White House, at the north entrance followed by a large ceremony on the south grounds.

The most dramatic and visible ceremonies on the north grounds, however, take place during a change of administration when the outgoing president and first lady receive the incoming president and first lady at the North Portico. After a brief reception in the White House, they depart for the inaugural ceremony at the Capitol along the north drive. The north entrance was the only entrance to the White House

for family, guests, staff, and visitors until 1902; today it is used most often when heads of state arrive for a State Dinner.

Pennsylvania Avenue in front of the White House, closed to traffic since the Oklahoma City bombing in 1995, was redesigned with new paving, lighting, tree plantings, and benches in 2004. Inaugural parades continue to be reviewed by presidential families from a reviewing stand constructed in front of the north fence every four years, and the American people continue to gather here to view the President's House and to express their political views.

Following President George W. Bush's second swearing in, the inaugural parade moves down Pennsylvania Avenue passing the reviewing stand on the the north side of the White House, 2005.

THE EASTER EGG ROLL

Once a year—on Easter Monday—young-sters are invited to an egg-rolling party on the South Lawn. It is the largest public event held annually on the White House grounds. In 1878 this event, held on the Capitol grounds for many years, was moved to the White House at the invitation of President Rutherford B. Hayes. Since then, only war and inclement weather have canceled the Easter Egg Roll. In recent decades, along with the Easter Bunny, cartoon characters and children's authors have participated.

On April 1, 2002, George W. Bush blew a whistle for the official start of the

A scene from the Easter Egg Roll held on the South Lawn in 1889 during the administration of President Benjamin Harrison.

Left: Thousands of eggs are dyed by White House chefs each year and used for the races and egg hunts.

Below: President and Mrs. Bush look on as the 2006 White House Easter Egg Roll begins.

White House Easter Egg Roll. Nearly twenty thousand children raced to scoot a hard-boiled egg across the lawn with a spoon, a race first introduced at the White House in the Nixon administration; all of the participants were declared winners, and each received a souvenir wooden egg bearing the signatures of the Bushes. White House chefs dye eleven thousand real eggs for the races and for the egg hunts.

In 2003, as thousands of America's military men and women were deployed in some aspect of the Iraq War or other missions overseas, President and Mrs. Bush decided that the Easter Egg Roll would be dedicated to children who had a parent—or in some cases, both parents—away from home serving their country. Thousands of children and their families enjoyed the delightful springtime tradition.

PRESIDENTS AT PLAY

Many presidents have set up recreational facilities on the grounds. Rutherford B. Hayes marked off a croquet court near the South Portico, where, a staff member wrote, clerks as well as the family "used to spend an hour now and then . . . over hard-fought games with mallet and ball."

There has been a tennis court on the South Lawn since the time of Theodore Roosevelt. The press called associates who joined him for a fast, tough game his "tennis Cabinet." Warren G. Harding practiced golf shots on the lawn and trained his Airedale, Laddie Boy, to retrieve the balls. Herbert Hoover exercised with his "Medicine-Ball Cabinet" before breakfast conferences. Harry Truman pitched horseshoes; Dwight Eisenhower improved his golf on a presidential putting green.

President Herbert Hoover plays volleyball with his "Medicine-Ball Cabinet," 1933.

Pitching horsehoes has
been a favorite sport of
several presidents including Harry S. Truman (left),
1952, and President
George H. W. Bush
(above), c. 1991.

President Dwight D.
Eisenhower practices
his swing on the south
grounds.

The first outdoor swimming pool was installed near the Oval Office for Gerald Ford. The Carter family enjoyed the pool, the tennis courts, and the bowling alley under the North Portico. Ronald Reagan had no opportunity to enjoy his favorite exercise, horseback riding, on the White House grounds. Both he and the first lady used exercise equipment installed in a Second Floor room. George H. W. Bush, an active president, added a horseshoe pit and a basketball half-court, and pursued jogging, golf, tennis, and swimming. During the Clinton administration, a quarter-mile jogging track was added, and the Eisenhower putting green was restored on the south grounds.

A lifelong baseball fan, George W. Bush transformed a portion of the South Lawn into a baseball field for a series of tee ball games for children each summer. On opening day 2001, the Memphis Red Sox and the Rockies, both Washington, D.C., Little League teams, batted and fielded for cheering fans. Every little slugger took home a souvenir baseball signed by the president. President Bush used the jogging track during his first term; now he rides his bicycle frequently, and he uses the residence gym daily when he is there.

Above: President Gerald R. Ford demonstrates his use of the new outdoor swimming pool to the media, 1975.

Left: Miss Beazley chases behind President George W. Bush as he exercises on his bicycle on the South Lawn, 2005.

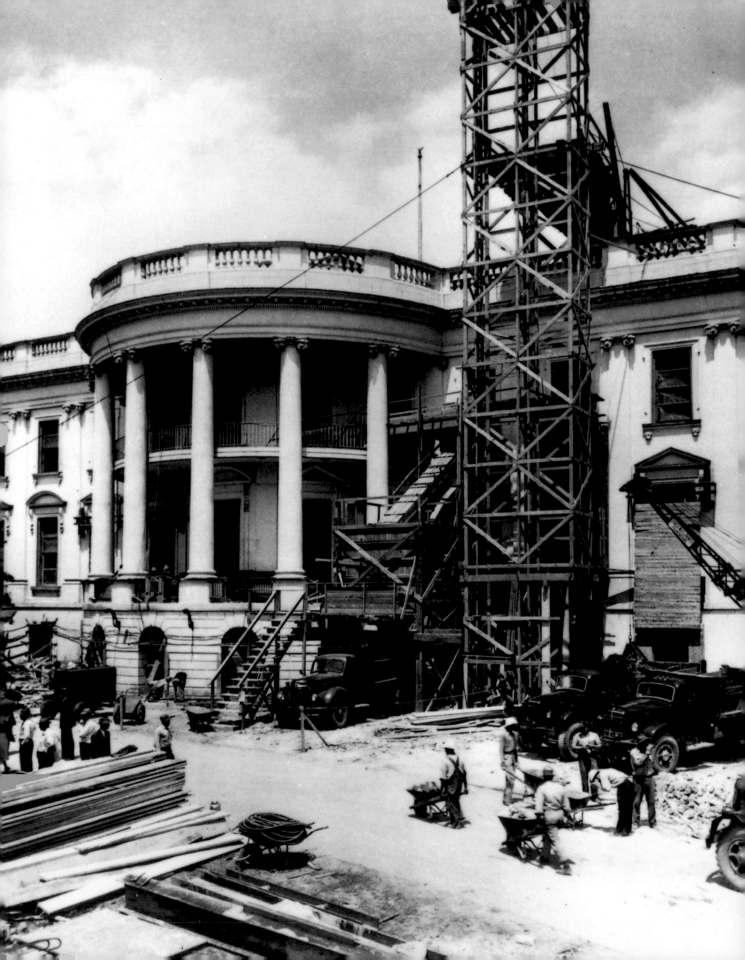

A House for the Ages

5

The President's House is the nation's house. It belongs to the people, and much care goes into its management. Over the years the house has been rebuilt, changed, expanded, and renovated, and those who have contributed to its permanency — its permanent place in the nation and in the hearts of the people — are many. They include builders and architects and stone masons and engineers as well as housekeepers and chefs. As Calvin Coolidge observed, presidents come and go, but those who care for the White House stay on. At a dinner in honor of the White House's two hundredth birthday, Gerald Ford paid tribute to the permanent staff of the White House residence: "To everyone who aids, comforts, and inspires a president and his loved ones," he said, and offered a toast "from our families to the White House family, to all you do to make this old house a home."

The South Front during the Truman renovation, April 1950. Demolition is in progress inside the house.

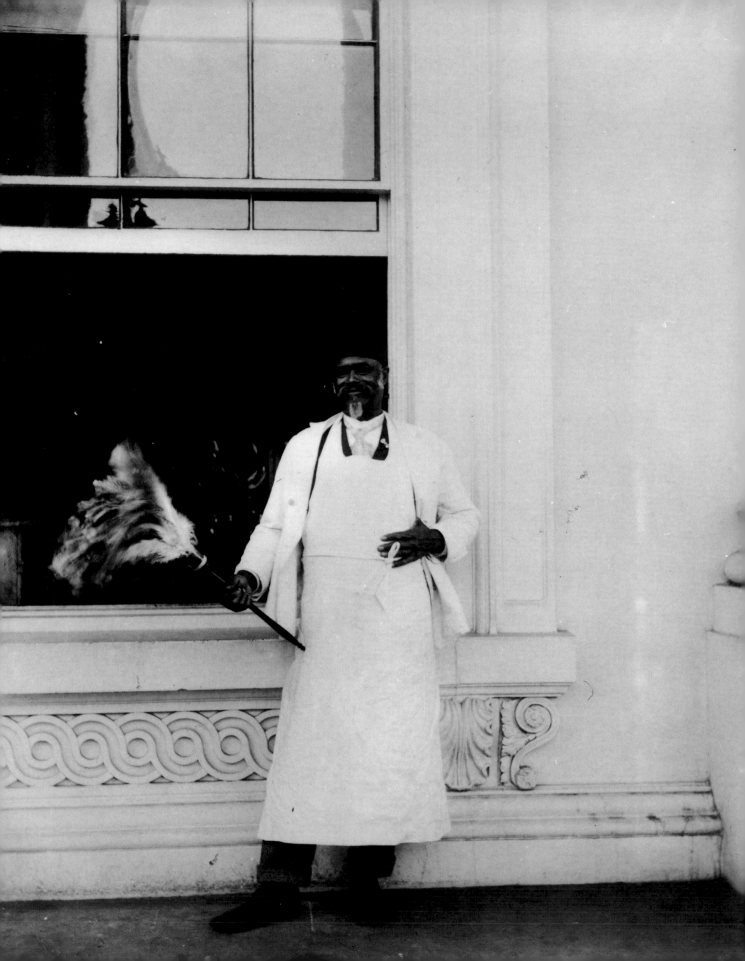

THE HOUSEHOLD STAFF

The chief executive and first lady who arrive at the White House today find a trained permanent staff ready to help manage what has now become a highly complex organization. In many ways the house resembles a small, well-run hotel. Furniture, works of art, bed and table linens, glasses, silverware, and china—state and informal—are all provided. Dedicated workers have and continue to assist the president and his family in making their home a comfortable one.

Today the combined domestic and maintenance staffs—most of whom carry on from one administration to another—number about ninety employees: florists, curators, housekeepers, chefs, butlers, carpenters, painters, and plumbers. At the head of these workers stands the chief usher; his job of coordinating and managing the manifold activities covers just about everything but ushering. If such a force seems large, consider how prodigious are the tasks for official events and how great the responsibility that goes with handling some of the nation's most valuable possessions. Consider, too, the normal wear and tear involved, and the cleaning needed after thousands of visitors pass through the State Rooms. The staff must keep the White House presentable and ready for the functions held there.

The big kitchen opening off the arched Ground Floor Corridor is any chef's dream of equipment and working space. In this gleaming white and stainless steel domain are grinders, slicers, choppers, mixers, electric ovens, and

Opposite: Housekeeper Jerry Smith wields a feather duster on the North Portico, c. 1900.

Above: President Harry S. Truman congratulates long-time employees, Sam Jackson and John Mays, 1950.

Above: Cook Dolly Johnson poses in the smaller of two White House kitchens, c. 1888–90.

Right: A cow named Pauline Wayne supplied milk during the Taft administration and grazed on the White House lawn behind the State, War, and Navy Building, c. 1909.

walk-in freezers. They help Executive Chef Cristeta Comerford, the first woman named to that position, and her assistants prepare State Dinners for as many as 140 guests, and hors d'oeuvres for a thousand or more.

Such expert aid and equipment would have appeared nothing short of miraculous to Abigail Adams, who wrote to her sister that she would have been pleased to have enough candles "lighting the apartments, from the kitchen to parlors and chambers." "The house was made habitable," she wrote to her daughter, but the main stairs were not yet up, not a single apartment had been finished, and bells for summon-

ing servants were "wholly wanting to assist us in this great castle."

Other first ladies also struggled with managing the house. Dolley Madison, a biographer noted, "superintended all her domestic arrangements before breakfast." And in the 1860s, an admiring woman correspondent described a morning chore performed by capable Martha Patterson, daughter of President Andrew Johnson, who would "don a calico dress and spotless apron, and then descend to skim the milk and attend the dairy." As recently as the Taft administration, a cow named Pauline Wayne supplied milk for the household and grazed on the White House lawn.

Above: Executive Chef Cristeta Comerford at work in the modern White House kitchen, 2005.

Above: The members of the Usher's Office, Dennis Freemyer, Gary Walters, Nancy Mitchell, Chris Emery, and Skip Allen, stand at the North Door prior to an event in 1990.

Opposite: White House clerks and messengers gather at the north entrance, c. 1890.

Until the early twentieth century the president had to pay for all of his and his family's daily needs, whether personal or in connection with official duties. The president even provided his own horses and carriages and was responsible for their upkeep. To be sure, Congress appropriated money for repairs and furnishings for the mansion, and to many the annual presidential salary of $25,000 must have seemed enough to take care of everything else. But the appropriations often varied with the whims of Congress, and the cost of maintaining a household that reflected the dignity of the nation worked a hardship on many presidents. Thomas Jefferson and James Monroe were later forced to sell land to pay debts accumulated during their White House years.

Jefferson's numerous and lavish gourmet dinners—the result of a habit he acquired in France of "mitigating business with dinner" virtually ate up his salary. In eight years his bills for wine alone came to nearly $11,000. And he once noted that when Congress was in session he needed a great deal more wine, especially champagne. Washington food costs were higher, too, than elsewhere. Jefferson's grocery bill often amounted to $50 a day—at a time when 75 cents for a turkey and $3 for a hog were considered high prices. In William Henry Harrison's time, White House life was so casual that the president sometimes did his own marketing, carrying his groceries home in a basket. Helen Taft hired the first housekeeper in 1909, to supervise the food buying and the preparation of meals for both the president's family and guests. Previously a steward had seen to routine marketing, and caterers met special requirements. Today, a storekeeper takes care of the daily marketing needs, and the Secret Service checks the purchases before delivery.

It was not until the Taft administration that Congress relieved presidents of having to pay the wages of house staff. John and Abigail Adams brought their own servants to the house in 1800; southern presidents,

Opposite: On their last morning in the White House, President and Mrs. Eisenhower bid farewell to the household staff, 1961.

Above: Members of the White House domestic staff from the Rutherford B. Hayes Administration, c. 1880.

including Thomas Jefferson, James Madison, James Monroe, Andrew Jackson, and Zachary Taylor, brought their slaves. These presidents often hired French or Belgium stewards or maîtres d'hôtel to arrange dinners and receptions. Madison's "body servant" or valet, Paul Jennings, wrote the first memoir by a member of the White House staff, *A Colored Man's Reminiscences of James Madison*. After the Civil War, the first official steward, hired by Andrew Johnson in 1866, was an African American, William Slade. Slade, who had been a messenger for Abraham Lincoln, was put in charge of the domestic management of the house.

Warren G. Harding was the first president for whom the government picked up the check for official entertaining. Congress also has recognized the advancing level of salaries in the United States, though the sums paid the chief executive have lagged behind those received by many corporation presidents. In 1873, effective with Ulysses S. Grant's second term, Congress raised the president's salary from $25,000 a year to $50,000. William Howard Taft, in 1909, became the first chief executive to earn $75,000. In 1949, Harry S. Truman was the first to receive $100,000. The annual salary is now $400,000. The president still must defray the first family's living expenses. He pays for their food, laundry, and dry cleaning, for their personal telephone calls, and for all their private parties.

IMPROVING THE WHITE HOUSE

Through the years, the latest home conveniences have added to the comfort in the President's House.

The building Jefferson moved into in 1801 may have been "big enough for two emperors, one pope, and the grand lama," as a satirist observed, but it lacked practical arrangements for the everyday management of a home. So the president added colonnaded wings on either side of

Four workmen pose in a large bathtub made for President William Howard Taft.

the mansion; they contained servants' quarters, storage and laundry areas, an icehouse, a meat house, a wine cellar, and a henhouse. Inside, the inventive Mr. Jefferson devised a set of revolving trays, called a dumbwaiter, built into the walls of his dining room. With this contrivance, guests could be served from outside the room without having butlers close enough to overhear their private conversations. "You need not speak so low," Jefferson once assured a nervous guest. "Our walls have no ears."

Probably the greatest inconvenience of the early White House was the lack of running water. In the few months John and Abigail Adams lived there, servants had to haul water from nearly half a mile away. Jefferson set up an attic cistern with a system of wooden pipes reaching through the floors for water closets. But it was not until 1833, in Andrew Jackson's second term, that a system of iron pipes brought in spring water to the east terrace and permitted the frontiersman to enjoy hot and cold showers.

Martin Van Buren put in a basement "reservoir" with a "double-forcing pump" to supply water for kitchen and bathing needs. He thereby added fuel to the political fires stoked by Congressman Charles Ogle. In the "Gold Spoon Oration" that accused the president of living in decadent luxury, Ogle ridiculed him as one who indulged in the Grecian and Roman "pleasures of the warm or tepid bath."

The precise date of the introduction of modern plumbing in the White House remains in doubt. But records show that in 1853 the family quarters had central plumbing and bathtubs with hot and cold running water. By 1876, water to several tubs and water closets was supplied by pipes connected to a 2,000-gallon tank in the attic.

The chronology of other improvements is clearer. In December 1848 the Polks became the first presidential couple to exchange oil lamps and candlelight for gas illumination. At a reception given soon after, the "brilliant jets suddenly vanished," leaving the guests in darkness— except in the Blue Room. There, Sarah Polk said with satisfaction, she had had the foresight to retain the "elegant chandelier," whose "wax candles were shedding their soft radiance." The Fillmores introduced a kitchen stove in the 1850s, new technology for the cook who had been preparing even the most lavish meals at a big, open fireplace filled with kettles, pots, skillets, hooks, and cranes.

From the start, the big rooms have been hard to heat. In the cold winter of 1800–1801, the chill in the house was caused by a scarcity of logs for the many fireplaces. "Shiver, shiver," Abigail Adams wrote, "surrounded with forests, can you believe that wood is not to be had, because people cannot be found to cut and cart it." "Hell itself couldn't warm that corner," Jackson later complained. A hot-air furnace was installed in the Ground Floor oval room in 1840 to heat the State Floor and Second Floor hall. The mansion's first central furnace—a coal-fueled, hot water and forced-air system—was installed in 1853, after Franklin Pierce moved in.

Accustomed to the fine surroundings of his Tennessee plantation, Andrew Jackson immediately sought appropriations from Congress to improve the mansion, which the legislators had allowed to fall into a shabby state during the John Quincy Adams administration.

As electricity was installed in the White House, gas fixtures were replaced with electric light bulbs. The Family Dining Room is pictured (above) in 1892 with a new chandelier in place of the gas fixture pictured in 1889 (right).

Throughout Jackson's two terms, a willing Congress provided him with nearly $50,000 to refurbish the house and to build the massive, rectangular North Portico to complement the gracefully curving south entrance added by Monroe. Before the end of Jackson's first year, the great East Room was at last completely and handsomely furnished to permit the ceremonial use for which it was originally planned. The president was particularly interested in having the Monroe chairs made for the room in 1817 repaired and reupholstered, according to one account, so that people would not be

kept "standing upon their legs as they do before kings and emperors."

When former Vice President Chester A. Arthur took office after the death of James Garfield in 1881, he began making some of the most drastic changes yet seen in the appearance of the mansion. "I will not live in a house like this," he said after inspecting the accumulation of mixed and battered furniture and ornaments. Nor did he. Arthur sold at public auction thirty barrels of china and twenty-four wagon-loads of discards and turned to Louis Comfort Tiffany to lavishly redecorate the mansion, including the famous Tiffany stained-glass screen on the formal State Floor.

President and Mrs. Benjamin Harrison introduced electric lighting but were timid about using it. Ike Hoover, who became chief usher during the Taft administration, began his forty-two-year White House career in 1891 by setting up the novel system. He wrote later that the Harrisons "were afraid to turn the lights on and off for fear of getting a shock."

President Chester A. Arthur made many changes to the White House decor, including the transformation of the Entrance Hall with the installation of a colored glass screen created by Louis Comfort Tiffany, c. 1882.

THE ROOSEVELT AND TRUMAN RENOVATIONS

The renovations made during President Theodore Roosevelt's administration included the introduction of steel beams to support the floors (opposite) and the addition of the West Wing (below), 1902.

As each renovation and improvement brought in more wires, pipes, and flues, walls and structural supports reflected the strain on the old house. The creaking noises that had bred ghost stories for years finally forced an engineering survey in 1948. The report disclosed that the structure "was standing up," as one investigator put it, "purely from habit." The alternatives: renovate it or tear it down.

The same issue had risen in 1902 after Theodore Roosevelt and his large family moved in following the death of William McKinley. But Roosevelt wanted to continue to live in the historic house. Edith Roosevelt asked the distinguished architect Charles McKim for his advice, and his recommendations for a complete renovation led to major changes in the interior and the functioning of the house. The Roosevelt renovation doubled the space allocated to the family living quarters and provided a new wing for the president and his staff, and a new area on the east for receiving guests. The White House and, with a few exceptions, much of the complex as it is today reflect the work of 1902.

The 1902 renovations had put severe stress on the building's structure, as had the weight of the raised roof that created Third Floor space for guests and service rooms in the Coolidge era. Backed by public pleas to save the White House in 1948, Congress provided funds to remove the interiors and reinstall them within the original shell. Inside, a skeleton of steel structural beams on a new concrete

Right: Carpenters lay a new wooden floor as the State Dining Room is reconstructed following the rebuilding of the interiors, 1952.

Opposite: The interior of the White House was gutted and rebuilt during the Truman administration. New concrete foundations were constructed beneath the eighteenth-century outer walls, 1950.

foundation assured the future of the house. In the end, many architectural modifications were made and little of the nineteenth-century or early twentieth-century interiors remained. Two levels of subbasements and service areas under the North Portico were constructed, and the Grand Staircase was substantially changed to open into the Entrance Hall. One of the first central air-conditioning systems in the country was installed to provide relief from Washington summers. When the work was completed in 1952, the house at last was "built for ages to come," as Abigail Adams had seen it in 1800. It also was supplied with comforts that would have startled Millard Fillmore, who called it his "temple of inconveniences."

The most radical renovation in White House history would provide a home for future presidents and their families.

The attic where Abraham Lincoln and Theodore Roosevelt's children had played was transformed into guest rooms for visiting friends and family. The Coolidges' "Sky Parlor," with its magnificent view to the south, became a Solarium. Presidents and their wives have found this bright room a pleasant spot for informal entertaining, or a place to relax and read, to listen to music, or to watch television. Children and adolescents have turned the room into a busy and happy place. Here was the Kennedy kindergarten; here Luci Johnson, surrounded by furniture she had painted, had her teenage hideaway. And here first family youngsters have exchanged news and confidences with their friends. In recent decades, the Ford, Carter, and Clinton families used the Solarium as a kind of second living room, more casual than the Second Floor sitting halls.

Of all the additions to the mansion's facilities, probably the most useful was the Second Floor dining room—the President's Dining Room—with its pantry and kitchen. By converting one of the bedroom suites of the Second Floor apartment into a dining room and kitchen, the Kennedys made it possible for the family to enjoy meals with guests in a homelike atmosphere instead of having to use the State Dining Room or the smaller original Family

Stone masons repair the walls of the South Portico prior to painting in 1997.

Dining Room on the State Floor. At one of the Nixons' dinner parties in this room, Alice Roosevelt Longworth surprised and amused her hosts and other guests when she suddenly exclaimed, "My goodness . . . this is the room where I had my appendix out." Studying wallpaper in the room that depicted scenes of the American Revolution during a small dinner in May 1981, Great Britain's Prince Charles good-naturedly chided President Ronald Reagan for seating him where he had to look at Lord Cornwallis's surrender at Yorktown.

The President's Dining Room is often used by the George W. Bushes for informal meals with family and close friends. The menus are usually light, healthy foods or regional specialties such as Mexican food. A large, beautiful painting by Georgia O'Keeffe entitled *Jimson Weed* dominates one wall. As Mrs. Bush explains, "When we came from Texas, we knew we wanted to bring with us something of the Southwest, and we were thrilled when the Georgia O'Keeffe Museum offered to lend us this painting."

Work on the White House is never truly finished. Renovation of the exterior stone walls, begun during the Carter years, was completed in 1996. It included the removal of some forty coats of paint, repair of the stone, and repainting. Now the same work continues on the East and West Wings and colonnades. The Reagan years saw an improved security system and the addition of a special visitors' entrance. Outside this entrance, East

Executive Avenue was transformed into a tree-lined pedestrian mall.

In the 1990s, an effort to make the White House more energy efficient included the most extensive overhaul of the mansion's heating, ventilating, and air-conditioning system since the Truman administration. A new roof was added, too. Hillary Clinton, with the advice of the Committee for the Preservation of the White House, oversaw the refurbishing of several of the formal spaces on the State Floor: the Blue Room, East Room, State Dining Room, Entrance Hall, and Cross Hall. Worn, faded fabrics in the Blue Room were replaced with brilliant sapphire ones, while the walls were repapered in a gold pattern with a blue-and-gold swag border. The East Room, used for press conferences, bill signings, concerts, and receptions, had long been uncarpeted. Three pale green-and-gold woven rugs were installed to soften the appearance of the room and to provide better acoustics for special events. The State Dining Room was painted a stone color in keeping with its 1902 Colonial Revival architectural paneling, and it received new floral-patterned draperies and a new carpet. New red damask draperies appeared at the north windows of the Entrance Hall, and the Cross Hall and Grand Staircase were freshly carpeted. Furniture was reupholstered. This effort was part of the continuous change that goes on in and around this house.

Many of the decorative pieces, like the furnishings and paintings in the family

Wallpaper is hung in the Blue Room during the refurbishment in 1995.

area known as the West Sitting Hall, have been there for years. Laura Bush believes that a particularly beautiful painting by Claude Monet, for example, has remained in the same prominent place in that room through recent administrations because it brings a peaceful air to a spot where first ladies often do their work and entertain visiting dignitaries. And two of her favorite pieces in the Center Hall have long been in the White House—a lovely portrait of *Ruth* by Thomas Eakins and a painting by Mary Cassatt, *Young Mother and Two Children.*

Mrs. Bush says that two of the first rooms she decorated in the residence were for the Bushes' children, Barbara and Jenna. "Their rooms have often been children's bedrooms. Chelsea Clinton, Amy

Carter, the Johnson girls, Tricia Nixon, and the Kennedy children used these rooms. I filled the shelves with our daughters' books and photos so that when they are here they will feel at home."

An avid reader and collector of books, Laura Bush sent the family's large personal library to the ranch, knowing that she and her family could take advantage of the splendid White House archives. "For years the American Booksellers Association has made a presentation to the White House

The refurbished Library pictured in 2007. The room is decorated in the style of the late Federal period and located on the Ground Floor of the White House.

of the 250 most popular titles during that president's term. I can go book-browsing here to my heart's content!" She keeps particularly interesting volumes on the residence shelves and in the guest rooms for the enjoyment of visitors. She also supported the recommendation of the Committee for the Preservation of the White House to update the books selected in the early 1960s for the Ground Floor White House Library. More than six hundred new publications reflecting recent scholarship were added. In 2006, the

Library and the Vermeil Room were refurbished with freshly painted walls, redesigned draperies and new upholstery.

In 1945, President Truman placed pieces associated with President Lincoln into the room that had served as Lincoln's office and Cabinet Room, later renamed the Lincoln Bedroom. Among the objects installed by President Truman is the massive carved rosewood bed purchased by Mary Todd Lincoln for the state guest room, and in which the Lincolns' third son, Willie, died in 1862. Little changed in the sixty years following the Truman renovation, and by 2002, the room showed its wear. Mrs. Bush requested the advice of the Committee for the Preservation of the White House to consider changes to the Lincoln Bedroom, and she worked with the committee to create a room that reflects the historic record and the styles of the 1860s. Replicas of the Lincoln-era marble mantel, draperies, and a carpet were reproduced, based on historic photographs and sketches drawn by the artist Francis B. Carpenter, who spent hours in the room in Lincoln's time when he was preparing studies for his work *The First Reading of the Emancipation Proclamation Before the Cabinet.* Pleased with the result, Mrs. Bush noted, "The committee's painstaking research and the fine workmanship of the wallpaper designers, rugmakers, marble workers, and other craftsmen are obvious to everyone who steps into this room. Visitors have a real sense of how the White House looked in Lincoln's day. The restoration is beautifully done."

First Lady Laura Bush and Curator William Allman observe work during the refurbishment of the Lincoln Bedroom.

The Lincoln Bedroom following the completion of the refurbishment, 2005.

TOURS AND TALES

President Truman conducts the first televised tour of the White House, 1952.

Whatever fate befalls the president, the presidency never dies. Perhaps that is why Americans never tire of stories about the men who have held this office and the historic building in which he works and lives with his family.

Visitors to the White House are always curious about the life-size Gilbert Stuart portrait of George Washington that dominates the East Room. It is the only object that has remained in the White House since before the British torched the building in 1814. That afternoon, as British troops approached Washington, Dolley Madison saved the portrait before she fled. James Madison had already left the city, to join the defending forces in Maryland. Mrs. Madison, in a letter to her sister, explained how she saved the painting. "Our kind friend, Mr. Carroll, has come to hasten my departure," she wrote, "and is in a very bad humor with me, because I insist on waiting until the large picture of Gen. Washington is secured, and it requires to be unscrewed from the wall. This process was found too tedious. . . . I have ordered the frame to be broken and the canvas taken out; it is done."

Millions turned on their television sets to follow the White House tours conducted by President Truman after the building's renovation in 1952, by Jacqueline Kennedy when she discussed her historical vision and showed off antiques and artwork acquired through her special historical project in 1962, and by Tricia Nixon when she took television viewers on the first public showing of many of the rooms

in the family living quarters. Included were glimpses of the family dining and sitting rooms and her mother's sitting room, in which she read and answered her mail, and the piano her father liked to play. She also described an incident in which Nixon built the flames so high in the fireplace of his private study adjoining the Lincoln Bedroom that an alarm sent White House firefighters rushing to the scene. There they found him placidly writing a speech before the open fire, which, Tricia explained, was one of his great pleasures.

In September 1989, George H. W. and Barbara Bush gave television viewers another personal tour of their family quarters. Then, in 1995, the Clintons treated millions of viewers to a look at the freshly refurbished Blue and East Rooms. After the President's House was closed to tours after the tragic events of September 11, 2001, Laura Bush led a special television program of the White House Christmas decorations and has done so each year since.

Mamie Eisenhower led one of the most unusual tours in 1959. Her guests were all children or descendants of former presidents, beginning with John Adams. Eight were sons and daughters of chief executives from Grover Cleveland to Dwight Eisenhower. History traveled with the party as past residents of the house moved upstairs and down, swapping anecdotes about how it was when they knew "life with father" here.

First Lady Jacqueline Kennedy checks a table set in the State Dining Room in preparation for her televised tour, which was aired by CBS in 1962.

Above: Tricia Nixon leads a televised tour through the family's living quarters and on to the Truman Balcony with Mike Wallace and Harry Reasoner, 1970.

Opposite: Visitors line the paths of the South Lawn during a garden tour, 1986.

Alice Roosevelt Longworth, daughter of TR, recalled the three circular Victorian ottomans, crowned by potted palms, that once stood in the East Room: "The tops in the center came off," she said, "and my brothers and sister would hide there." Helen Taft Manning, daughter of William Howard Taft, remembered that her mother found the huge Lincoln bed too depressing a symbol for sleep; she relegated it to the attic. Eleanor Wilson McAdoo, daughter of Woodrow Wilson, wanted to quash the myth that pictured her father as "an intellectual snob" and "a grim old Presbyterian." In fact, she said, he was "our most amusing and gay companion."

All of the home-comers but one received a surprise when the group made its way down the center hall to the Monroe Room that contained copies of President James Monroe's furniture, including a replica of the desk on which he signed his famous Monroe Doctrine. Pausing before this desk, Laurence Gouverneur Hoes, Monroe's great-great-grandson, pressed a panel that opened to reveal a secret compartment even Mrs. Eisenhower had not known about. Such a compartment, it turned out, had been discovered in the original desk in 1906, and young Hoes had been indirectly responsible for the find. As a small boy, he had somehow damaged this treasured family possession, and its repair had disclosed the hidden space. In it lay priceless letters written by Thomas Jefferson, James Madison, John Marshall, and Lafayette.

In the years since September 11, 2001, those wishing to visit the President's House to see the State Rooms must make advance reservations through their congressional representatives. They may also visit the White House website (www.whitehouse.gov) to view special tours of the White House, including the Oval Office conducted by President George W. Bush and the Diplomatic Reception Room by First Lady Laura Bush. Additional historical material about the White House and presidents and their families is available at the White House Historical Association website (www.whitehousehistory.org).

The Best of Blessings

Conclusion

Portraits of those whose lives are forever interwoven with memories of the White House hang throughout the State Rooms. Their attire, from knee breeches to modern dress, recalls the many eras the house has known, as presidents moved to shape and be shaped by events, and to leave on the American character the imprint of their philosophy and words. Thomas Jefferson wrote, "Our liberty can never be safe but in the hands of the people themselves." Abraham Lincoln said, "With malice toward none" and showed compassion that might have helped heal the wounds after the fratricidal war, had he survived. "Speak softly and carry a big stick," was a favorite motto of Theodore Roosevelt, who launched the building of the Panama Canal, won a formidable reputation for "trust-busting," and sent sixteen battleships of the United States Navy on parade around the world. A long list of memorable phrases emerged during the White House years of Franklin D. Roosevelt, the only president elected to four terms. Best remembered, perhaps, are, "The only thing we have to fear is fear itself," "New Deal," and "the Four Freedoms."

In reflecting on his years in the presidency, Harry S. Truman spoke to the American people in his farewell address in 1953. "So, as I empty the drawers of this desk, and as Mrs. Truman and I leave the White House, we have no regret. We feel we have done our best in the public service. I hope and believe we have contributed to the welfare of this Nation and to the peace of the world." John F. Kennedy eloquently expressed the symbolic meaning of the White House in American history. "I consider history—our history—to be a source of strength to us here in the White House and to all the American people. Anything which dramatizes the

Opposite: President Abraham Lincoln's portrait is pictured in 1948 above the marble mantel in the State Dining Room that President Franklin D. Roosevelt had inscribed with a blessing for the house written by President John Adams in 1800.

great story of the United States—as I think the White House does—is worthy of the closest attention and respect by Americans who live here and who visit here and who are part of our citizenry."

Whether they come for social occasions, work, or sightseeing, visitors find inscribed on the mantel of the State Dining Room a benediction and an expression of hope from the earliest days of the republic. The words were taken from a letter written by President John Adams on his second night in the new mansion. Franklin Roosevelt had them cut into the mantel.

I pray Heaven to bestow
the best of Blessings on this House
and all that shall hereafter inhabit it.
May none but honest and wise men
ever rule under this roof.

Illustration Credits

All images are copyrighted by the White House Historical Association unless listed below. The illustrations on pages ii, 5, 6, 41, and 46 are in the White House Collection and the images of these illustrations are copyrighted by the WHHA.

Illustration Credits key:

LOC – Library of Congress

NARA – National Archives

WH – White House Photo

v	LOC
vi	WH
x	Time and Life Pictures/Getty Images
xii	LOC
2	LOC
7	Albert H. Small Collection, Number 44
8	Rutherford B. Hayes Presidential Center
9	Harry S. Truman Library; Associated Press
10–13	LOC
15	LOC; Jimmy Carter Library
16	White House Collection Gift of Graham R. Hodges; LOC
17	NARA; WH
18	Franklin D. Roosevelt Presidential Library and Museum
19	Gerald R. Ford Presidential Library and Museum
20	Ronald Reagan Library; Corbis
21–22	WH
24	LOC; NARA
25	John F. Kennedy Presidential Library and Museum
26	Lyndon Baines Johnson Presidential Library and Museum; Nixon Presidential Materials
27	George Bush Presidential Library; William J. Clinton Presidential Library; WH
28	Jimmy Carter Library
29–30	Ronald Reagan Library
33	Perley's Reminiscences
34–35	LOC
40	Perley's Reminiscences
43	George Eastman House
44–45	LOC
52	New-York Historical Society
53	Bettmann Archives
54	NARA
55–56	LOC
57	Franklin D. Roosevelt Presidential Library and Museum; Wide World
58	Harry S. Truman Library
59	WHHA
60	John F. Kennedy Presidential Library and Museum
61	Bettmann/Corbis; Gerald R. Ford Presidential Library and Museum
64	Ronald Reagan Library; George Bush Presidential Library
65	William J. Clinton Presidential Library
66–69	WH
70	Jimmy Carter Library
71	Lyndon Baines Johnson Presidential Library and Museum; Courtesy of Betty Monkman
72	Gerald R. Ford Presidential Library and Museum; George Bush Presidential Library; William J. Clinton Presidential Library
73–83	WH
84	John F. Kennedy Presidential Library and Museum
85	William J. Clinton Presidential Library
86	John F. Kennedy Presidential Library and Museum
87	Nixon Presidential Materials
88–89	WH
90	LOC
93	Franklin D. Roosevelt Presidential Library and Museum
95	Nixon Presidential Materials
96	WHHA; George Bush Presidential Library
97	Jimmy Carter Library; WHHA
98	Wally McNamee / Corbis
99	WH
100	Harper's Bazaar
101	LOC
103	NARA
105–11	LOC

112	NARA	158	Mrs. John M. Scott, Jr., Mobile, Alabama
113	Dwight D. Eisenhower Library	159	Huntington Library, San Marino, California
114	John F. Kennedy Presidential Library and Museum	161	Historical Society of Washington, DC
115	Nixon Presidential Materials	162	LOC
116	Jimmy Carter Library; George Bush Presidential Library	163	John F. Kennedy Presidential Library and Museum
117	WH	164–66	WH
118	LOC; Lyndon Baines Johnson Presidential Library and Museum; Bettmann / Corbis; Jimmy Carter Library	167	William J. Clinton Presidential Library
		168	Rutherford B. Hayes Presidential Center
		169	LOC
119	Bettmann / Corbis; Bettmann / Corbis; William J. Clinton Presidential Library	171	Dwight D. Eisenhower Library; John F. Kennedy Presidential Library and Museum; Jimmy Carter Library
120	LOC		
121	James Monroe Law Library	172	Lyndon Baines Johnson Presidential Library and Museum; Jimmy Carter Library
122–26	LOC		
127	WHHA; Nixon Presidential Materials	173	William J. Clinton Presidential Library; Getty Images
128	LOC	174	Bettmann/Corbis
129	Kiplinger Washington Collection	175	LOC
130	Harper's Weekly	177	George Bush Presidential Library; WH; WH
132	Kiplinger Washington Collection	178	Wally McNamee / Corbis
133	Rutherford B. Hayes Presidential Center	179	WH
134	Ralph E. Becker Collection of Political Americana, Smithsonian Institution	180	LOC
		181	WH
135	Bettmann / Corbis	182	Harper & Row
136	NARA	183	WH; LOC
137	Associated Press; Corbis	184	United Press International
138	Dwight D. Eisenhower Library	185	Gerald R. Ford Presidential Library and Museum; WH
140	LOC		
141	Theodore Roosevelt Collection, Houghton Library, Harvard University	186	Harry S. Truman Library
		188	LOC
142	Lyndon Baines Johnson Presidential Library and Museum	189	Harry S. Truman Library
		190	WHHA; LOC
143	WH	191	WH
144	Culver Service Photograph	192	LOC
145	LOC	193	WH
146	NARA	194	Rutherford B. Hayes Presidential Center
147	Getty Images	195	Edward Clark
148	Lyndon Baines Johnson Presidential Library and Museum	196	Culver Service Photograph
		198–99	LOC
149	Dwight D. Eisenhower Library	200–201	Sagamore Hill National Historic Site
150	Jimmy Carter Library	202	Abbie Rowe, National Park Service
151	Ronald Reagan Library	203	Harry S. Truman Library
152	WH	206	WH
153	George Bush Presidential Library; William J. Clinton Presidential Library	207	WH; WHHA
		208	Harry S. Truman Library (EPG International)
154	WH	209	Associated Press
155	Jimmy Carter Library; WH	211	Associated Press
156	LOC		

INDEX

Italics indicate an illustration